IMAGES
of America

JEWISH DENVER
1859–1940

IMAGES
of America

JEWISH DENVER
1859–1940

Jeanne E. Abrams, Ph.D.

ARCADIA
PUBLISHING

Published by Arcadia Publishing
Charleston, South Carolina

Printed in the United States of America

Library of Congress Catalog Card Number: 2007933015

For all general information contact Arcadia Publishing at:
Telephone 843-853-2070
Fax 843-853-0044
E-mail sales@arcadiapublishing.com
For customer service and orders:
Toll-Free 1-888-313-2665

Visit us on the Internet at www.arcadiapublishing.com

*In memory of Peryle Hayutin Beck, Marjorie Hornbein, and Milt
Morris; in gratitude for their extraordinary dedication in preserving the
history of the Colorado Jewish community.*

CONTENTS

ACKNOWLEDGMENTS

The publication of Images of America: *Jewish Denver* affords the opportunity to showcase the rich collection of historical photographs from the Ira M. and Peryle Hayutin Beck Memorial Archives of Rocky Mountain Jewish History, part of Special Collections, Penrose Library and the Center for Judaic Studies, University of Denver. The Beck Archives was established in 1976 under the direction of Dr. Stanley M. Wagner, then director of the University of Denver's Center for Judaic Studies. Dr. Wagner's vision was central to the archive's development, and it was initiated with a generous grant by Peryle Beck in memory of her late husband, Ira M. Beck, a prominent Denver businessman devoted to cultural arts and Jewish communal life. Soon others were convinced of the importance of documenting the Jewish experience in the region, and before long, the Rocky Mountain Jewish Historical Society (RMJHS) was born. For more than 30 years, the Beck Archives and the RMJHS have worked in tandem to preserve and publicize the history of Colorado's Jewish community. The archives contain a variety of materials, including private papers, institutional records, oral histories, memorabilia, and evocative, vintage photographs.

Over the years, volunteers and contributors too numerous to mention have supported the work of the Beck Archives and the RMJHS, but several names stand out in particular: the late Peryle Beck, Marjorie Hornbein, Dr. John Livingston, Milton and Jean Morris, and Faye Schayer made the preservation and dissemination of the history of Colorado's Jewish community a central part of their lives. Belle Marcus, the energetic first director, put the institution on firm footing. It has been my privilege to serve as director for more than 25 years, and I look forward to being able to contribute to further growth.

My gratitude goes to Hannah Carney at Arcadia Publishing for her wise guidance. At the University of Denver, the staff at the CJS and Dean Nancy Allen have given their customary encouragement to the project, as have the dedicated board members of the RMJHS. I am especially grateful to my colleague Thyria Wilson and loyal volunteer Elliot Simonberg for expertly preparing the photographs for publication. Most importantly, I thank my supportive and loving family for making all my endeavors worthwhile.

Unless otherwise noted, all photographs are courtesy of the Ira M. and Peryle H. Beck Memorial Archives, Special Collections, Penrose Library and the Center for Judaic Studies, University of Denver.

INTRODUCTION

Colorado was still an untamed wilderness when the discovery of gold near Pike's Peak in 1858 brought the area to the nation's attention. By the spring of 1859, fortune seekers began to arrive in droves. Jews also took part in the quest. Jewish settlers arrived in Colorado as early as the 1850s, but there was no lasting Jewish community as such until the early 1870s when the first Jewish organizations and synagogues were formally established. The first Jewish settlers in the Denver area, primarily of Central European or German origin, came to Colorado in search of freedom, new opportunities on the frontier, and wealth. They were typical of the first Jewish settlers in the region—generally young, unmarried, of German descent, and entering businesses dealing with the distribution of goods. The open and expanding American economy before and after the Civil War contributed to the success of these enterprising pioneers, as did their merchandising experience and Jewish networks of credit that stretched back to the East Coast.

The unpredictability of gold mining and a growing demand for supplies encouraged many of these pioneer Jewish "1859ers" to establish small businesses in new towns and mining camps throughout Colorado. Their arrival marked the beginning of Denver's and Colorado's established Jewish community. During the next two decades, they settled in places throughout the state such as Leadville, Cripple Creek, Aspen, Trinidad, Colorado Springs, Pueblo, and Central City, but before long, Denver emerged as the main hub. In Southern Colorado, Jewish men were active in commerce from the earliest days of the Anglo entrance into that traditionally Hispanic area. They came via the Santa Fe Trail. Farther north in Pueblo and Colorado Springs, Jews began to arrive as early as the 1860s. Jewish brothers Burton and Charles Myers operated a hotel in Colorado Springs as early as 1864. Burton's wife later recalled that it was "a typical wild west hostelry where liquors were sold; card games ran all night."

As the early Jewish pioneer men married, often importing their brides from back east, and as children were born, the fledgling towns of Colorado began to stabilize. The Jewish community also began to establish a more permanent structure beginning with a pioneer Jewish burial society in Denver to ensure that their co-religionists were buried in accordance with Jewish tradition. Before long Jewish benevolent societies, a synagogue, and charitable groups began to appear on the horizon. While Jewish men often concentrated on city building, the women were instrumental in community building. Many of Colorado's Jewish women were involved in social welfare and reform both within and outside of the Jewish community and took central roles in helping to ensure Jewish continuity through support of synagogues, Jewish charitable institutions, education, and Jewish practices within the home. Frances Wisebart Jacobs, for example, became an icon in philanthropy throughout the entire Denver community, and she was later honored by a stained-glass window in the state capitol building for her notable work to improve conditions for the poor and sick in early Denver. Seraphine Pisko and Ray David were later closely involved in Jewish settlement work among the East European Russian immigrants and were appointed to prominent civic positions as well. By 1877, there were approximately 422 Jews living in Colorado, around 260 of them residing in Denver. Twenty years later, Colorado's Jewish population had risen to 1,500 with the majority living in Denver.

By the 1880s, as Denver's climate became known throughout the country as one favorable for curing respiratory diseases, tuberculosis in particular, people flocked to Colorado for their health. Soon Colorado was known popularly as the "World's Sanatorium," and the state became a mecca for consumptives, as tuberculosis was also commonly known. Jews, many from the garment industries of the East Coast, came to Denver in search of a cure for tuberculosis. Eventually, two national hospitals, the National Jewish Hospital for Consumptives (NJH) and the Jewish Consumptives' Relief Society (JCRS), were established by the Denver Jewish community to take care of their health needs and serve the community as a whole. Inspired by Frances Wisebart Jacobs, and with the financial assistance of Denver's acculturated, more affluent Reform Jews and the International Order of B'nai B'rith, NJH opened its doors in 1899 to Jews and Gentiles alike with early-stage tuberculosis, although the majority of patients for many years were East European Jews. Founded by a group of poor East European immigrants, the JCRS was opened in 1904 to treat patients in all stages of the disease and to offer patients a more traditional Jewish environment. Formally nonsectarian, the vast majority of consumptives at the JCRS sanatorium were also Russian Jews. In Europe, most of these immigrant Russian Jews had resided in the prescribed Pale of Settlement, comprised of Russian Poland, Lithuania, Byelorussia, and the Ukraine.

Other East European Jews began arriving in significant numbers after the Russian pogroms of 1881 and increasing economic deprivation and religious discrimination in their homeland. In addition, a large percentage of the health seekers who came to Denver were East European Jews who flocked to Denver after 1900 and significantly augmented the state's Jewish population and helped grow Denver's Jewish community. By 1907, Colorado's Jewish population numbered 6,500 Jewish citizens, with around 5,000 residing in Denver. The East European Jews settled primarily in Denver's west-side Colfax community, a predominantly Orthodox Jewish enclave filled with small shuls, kosher bakeries, meat markets, and grocery stores, which many compared to New York City's famous Lower East Side. It was some time before the German and Russian Jew factions, so different in many respects, melded into a cooperating, cohesive community. Jewish women from both groups were crucial to the survival of early communities and made distinct contributions not only in shaping Jewish communal life and ensuring Jewish continuity in Denver, but outside the Jewish community as well.

As the years passed, significant numbers of Jews of both East and Central European origins established businesses all over the state, providing goods and services to miners and ranchers. While the towns prospered, so did the Jews. However, when the gold ran out, most of the Jews left and settled in Denver or other large communities like Colorado Springs and Pueblo where they could more easily connect with a Jewish community and synagogues, and enjoy the amenities of life in a larger town. In Denver and in numerous small towns throughout the state, these Jewish pioneers and their descendants have played a vital role as prominent political, business, religious, social, and cultural leaders of the growing communities. The seeds of Jewish tradition and civic responsibility were planted and nurtured by Colorado's early Jewish pioneers, and today Denver's Jewish community continues to flourish.

One

DENVER'S JEWISH PIONEERS

Frustrated by centuries of discrimination, many Jews thrived in the generally benign and welcoming environment of the American West. The relative absence of anti-Semitism and the fluid social structure in the newly established Colorado boomtowns enabled many of the Jewish pioneers to enter politics, society, and business with more ease than Jews had known in other areas. As an "instant city," Denver welcomed Jewish men and women as a stabilizing influence who helped uphold morality and order in the new settlement, and brought a measure of culture to the rough frontier town. Several of the original Jewish 1859ers took a prominent role in early Denver. For example, Fred Zadek Salomon became the manager of the first general store in the city, while merchant Abraham Jacobs served as the secretary for the watershed meeting that merged the towns of Denver and Auraria into Denver City.

Denver's early pioneer Jews, men and women, soon founded synagogues, civic and charitable institutions, fraternal organizations, and hospitals, and became respected members of the growing community as they worked together with members of other religious and ethnic groups to put Denver on the national map. As they developed their own Jewish communal institutions, which fostered Jewish identity and activities, they also played a significant role in the development of Colorado and the Rocky Mountain West.

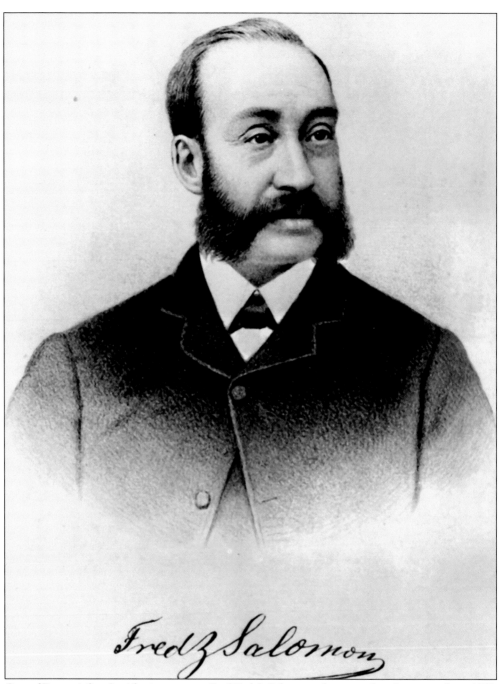

One of Denver's first Jewish pioneers was Fred Zadek Salomon who arrived in Auraria in June 1859. In short order, he became the manager of the first general mercantile company in Colorado. In partnership with gentile J. B. Doyle, the Prussian-born Salomon began the enterprise with $30,000 worth of goods. A popular figure in early Denver society, Fred Salomon was elected treasurer of the Denver Chamber of Commerce in 1860, was appointed territorial treasurer, and also served as an early Denver city councilman. (Courtesy of the Denver Public Library, Western History Collection.)

Pictured here is the early Salomon Brothers Grocery in Denver. Fred's brother Hyman Salomon was instrumental in bringing supplies to the South Park, Colorado, mining district near Fairplay, and the two were later joined by a third brother, Adolph Salomon, who became a trustee of the early Greeley, Colorado, colony. (Courtesy of the Denver Public Library, Western History Collection.)

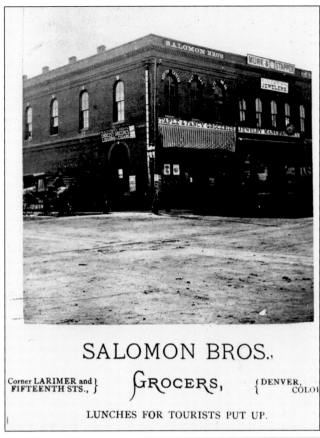

SALOMON BROS.,

Corner LARIMER and }
FIFTEENTH STS., }

GROCERS,

{ DENVER,
{ COLO!

LUNCHES FOR TOURISTS PUT UP.

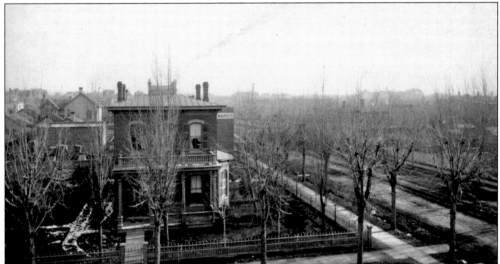

Abraham Jacobs, another of the 1859ers, opened a grocery store in Denver with a non-Jewish partner, Albert Buddee, and served on Denver's first city council. It was Jacobs who served as the secretary of the famous 1860 moonlight meeting when the towns of Denver and Auraria were united under the name of Denver City. Pictured here is the Denver residence of Abraham and Frances Wisebart Jacobs at Sixteenth and Welton Streets.

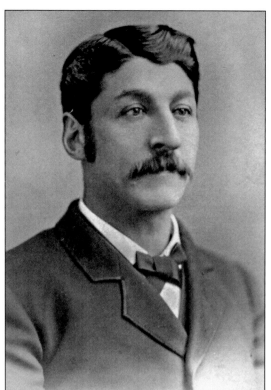

For a time, Abraham Jacobs moved his store to Central City, Colorado, where he went into partnership with Benjamin Wisebart, pictured here. Wisebart was elected mayor of Central City in 1876 and also became Jacobs's brother-in-law when Abraham married Frances Wisebart in 1863.

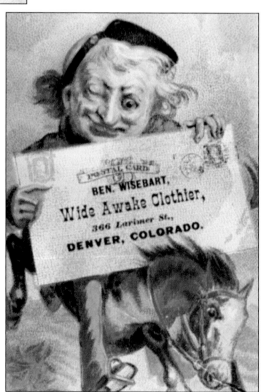

Shown here is an advertisement for Benjamin Wisebart's Denver clothing store.

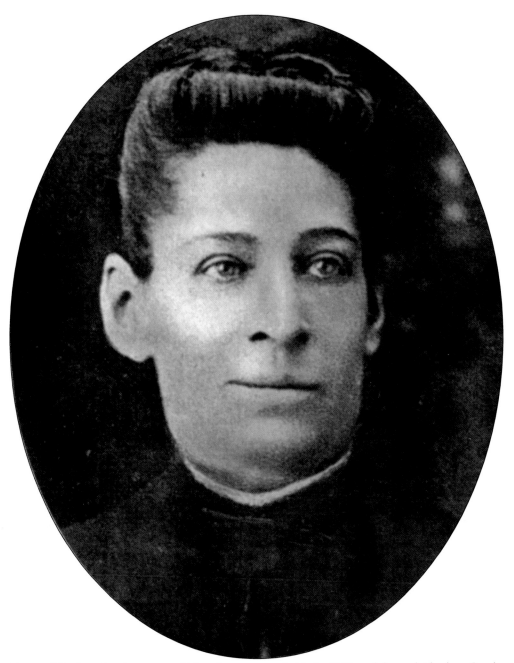

Frances Wisebart Jacobs came to Colorado as a young bride in 1863, and she and Abraham Jacobs made their first home in Central City. After the family relocated to Denver, she became active in the local Jewish and general community and was known nationally as Denver's "Mother of Charities" for her central role in philanthropy. She was an officer on several charitable organizations and helped to found both the National Jewish Hospital for Consumptives and the Denver Charity Organization Society, the forerunner of what became the national United Way.

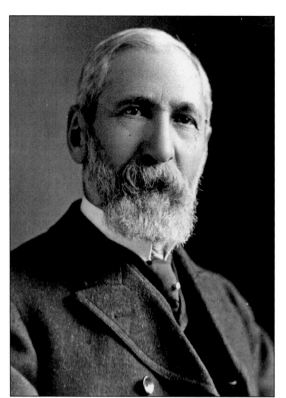

In 1859, shoe and boot merchant Leopold Mayer traveled 600 miles by foot beside his ox team to enter what was to become Denver. Active in both the Jewish and general community, he served for three terms as a Denver city councilman in the early 1860s.

Leopold Mayer later moved with his family to Saguache, Colorado, where he established a store and bank, pictured here. His Jewish partner in Saguache, Isaac Gotthelf, served as a representative in the state legislature from the southwestern part of Colorado from 1876 until 1881, and Gotthelf became speaker of the house in 1879.

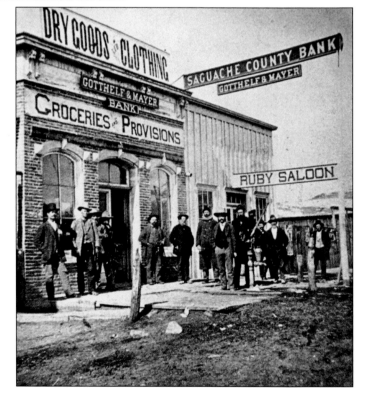

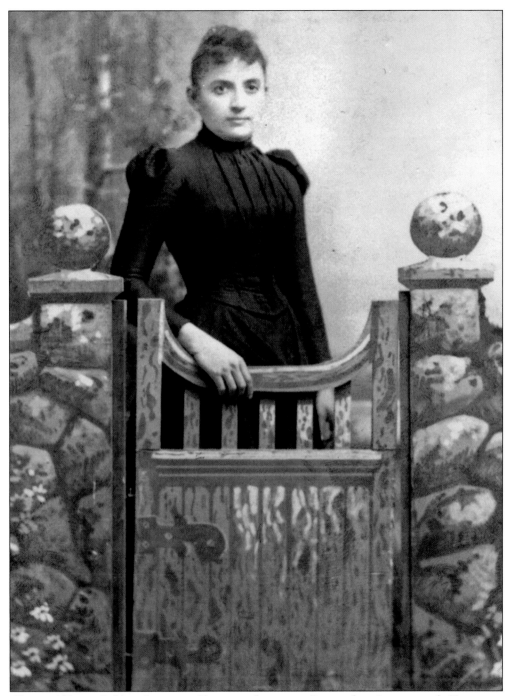

Clara and Henry Goldsmith migrated by covered wagon to Denver from Leavenworth, Kansas, in 1859 with relatives. Clara died in childbirth in 1860, and her new daughter, pictured here, was the first Jewish female baby born in Denver and was named Clara after her mother. Clara Goldsmith was raised by her aunt and uncle Rosa and Abraham Goldsmith as two sisters had married two brothers. The death of the elder Clara Goldsmith was the impetus behind the organization of Denver's first Jewish burial society.

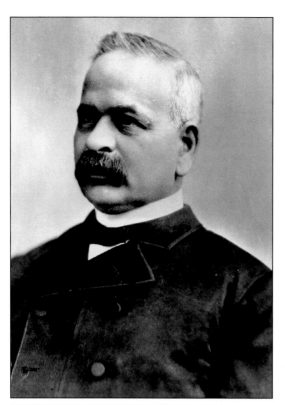

Brothers Wolfe and Julius Londoner began business in California Gulch, Colorado, as the area around Leadville was known in the 1860s. The brothers moved to Denver in about 1865 and soon opened a grocery store on Arapahoe Street called Londoner and Brother. Wolfe Londoner, pictured here, waged a controversial campaign for mayor of Denver in 1888 and was elected by a slim margin. He served as mayor from 1889 to 1891 when he was forced to resign due to accusations of election irregularities. He was later exonerated personally by the Colorado Supreme Court in 1891. (Courtesy of the Denver Public Library, Western History Collection.)

Mr. & Mrs. M. Hattenbach

request the pleasure of your company

to celebrate the confirmation of their son

Nathan,

on Sunday evening, June 14th, 1891, at their

home, 2245 Stout Street.

Denver,   =   =   Colorado.

Grocer Michael Hattenbach arrived in Central City in 1863 and moved to Denver in 1870. He became an active leader in Denver's B'nai B'rith, as well as a founder of Congregation Emanuel along with Louis Anfenger and Charles Schayer. Shown here is an invitation to a party given by Mr. and Mrs. Hattenbach celebrating the confirmation of their son Nathan in 1891.

Dr. John Elsner, shown here in a formal portrait, was Denver's first Jewish physician and led a wagon train into Colorado in 1866. He was instrumental in the establishment of Denver's first general hospital and also traveled the region as a *mohel* to perform the traditional Jewish rite of circumcision while conducting a busy private practice. (Courtesy of the Denver Public Library, Western History Collection.)

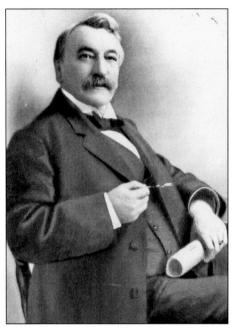

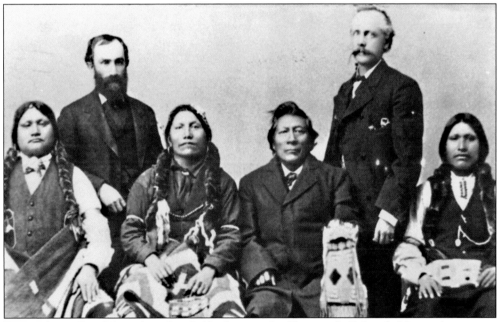

Russian-born Otto Mears (standing left), photographed here with Colorado Native Americans, emerged as one of Colorado's leading citizens. In 1865, Mears arrived in Colorado where he established a general store and gristmills in Conejos. Mears became known as the "Pathfinder" as he organized the buildings of roads and railroads through treacherous mountain canyons. He served in the Colorado House of Representatives from 1885 to 1886. Fluent in the Ute language, he also served as an Indian commissioner. Later as a prominent Denver citizen, Mears was appointed to the state board of capitol managers, and it is Mears who suggested the gold plating of the dome of the state capitol building. He is honored by a stained-glass window in the senate chamber of the building. (Courtesy of the Colorado Historical Society.)

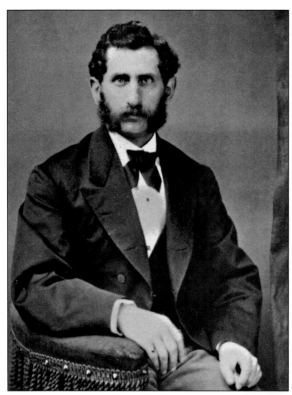

In 1865, Charles M. Schayer and his bride, Ricka Saft, pictured here, endured a seven-week journey by covered wagon to the Colorado Territory. Like so many of the early entrepreneurs, Charles Schayer took a prominent role in Colorado's Jewish community and served as an early lay rabbi at Congregation Emanuel. The Schayer name was to be interwoven into the thread of Colorado Jewish history over five generations.

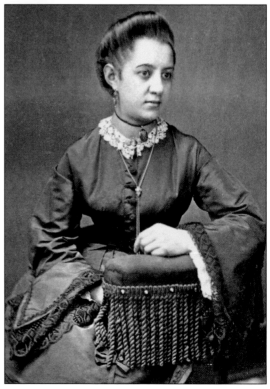

Charles Schayer came to join his brother Simon and established the Schayer wholesale wine and liquor business with a branch in the silver boomtown of Leadville, Colorado. This is a photograph of the early Denver store.

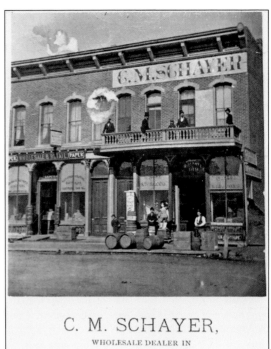

C. M. SCHAYER,

WHOLESALE DEALER IN

LIQUORS, WINES AND CIGARS

409 BLAKE STREET, DENVER, COL.

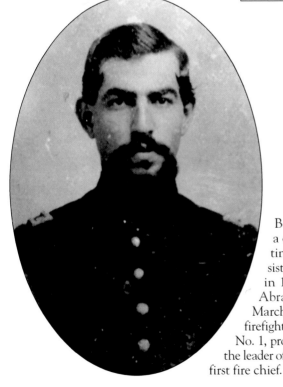

Born in Ohio, Philip Trounstine served as a captain in the Civil War, as shown in this tintype. Trounstine married Mollie Wisebart, sister of Frances Wisebart Jacobs, in Cincinnati in 1866 and later worked as the manager of Abraham Jacobs's Denver clothing store. In March 1866, Trounstine volunteered as a Denver firefighter as part of the Hook and Ladder Company No. 1, probably the first fire station in Colorado. As the leader of the company, he became, in effect, Denver's first fire chief.

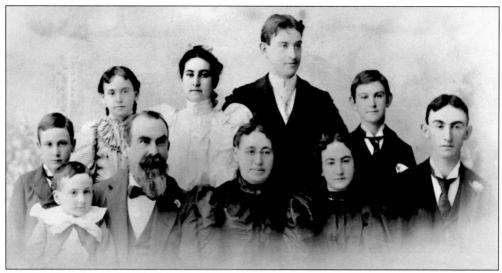

Louis Anfenger was typical of the young Jewish men who migrated to the Colorado Territory in the state's formative years. Born in Bavaria, Anfenger came to the United States in the 1850s and moved west in 1870 to seek his fortune. He started as a clerk and became a highly successful businessman in the area of real estate, as well as a member of the Denver Chamber of Commerce, and was later elected to the state legislature in the 1880s. He built a stately house at Champa Street and Twenty-ninth Street for his wife, Louise Schlesinger Anfenger, and their large family, pictured here in about 1890. Anfenger was a founder and supporter of Congregational Emanuel, the local B'nai B'rith, and National Jewish Hospital.

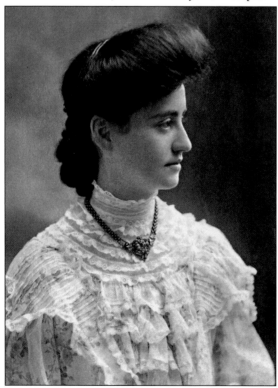

This c. 1900 photograph is of Louis and Louise Anfenger's daughter Fannie as a young woman, dressed in an elaborate gown.

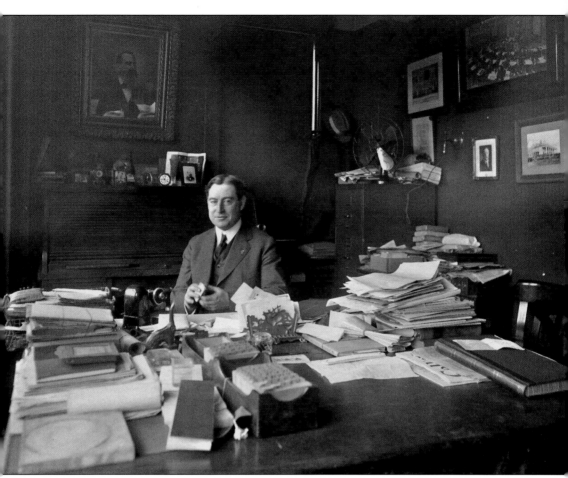

It is said that Congregation Emanuel was founded at the *bris* or circumcision ceremony of Milton Anfenger, the eldest son of Louis and Louise Anfenger. Pictured here at his desk *c.* 1920, Milton became a successful attorney and leader in Denver. He was a lifetime board member of National Jewish Hospital and wrote a book about its early history. Anfenger was active in state politics and was elected to the Colorado state senate in 1904. For nearly a decade in the 1920s, he became the owner of the Denver Bears baseball club.

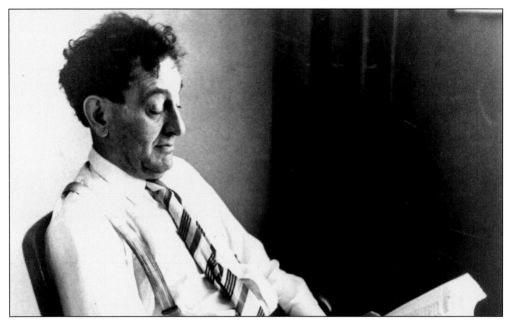

The son of East European Jewish immigrants, Philip Hornbein, photographed here in 1938, began his law career in Cripple Creek at the turn of the 20th century and became one of Denver's most outstanding Jewish leaders. He was known for his brilliance as a trial lawyer and served as state chairman of the state's Democratic party in the 1930s. With his marriage to Flora Anfenger in 1905, Hornbein became part of the staunchly Republican Anfenger family. He was a founder of Denver's Zionist movement and a supporter of the Jewish Consumptives' Relief Society (JCRS) sanatorium. Hornbein is said to have looked upon the law as a calling rather than a profession. Known as a defender of the underdog, he also led the fight against the Ku Klux Klan when it flourished in Colorado in the 1920s.

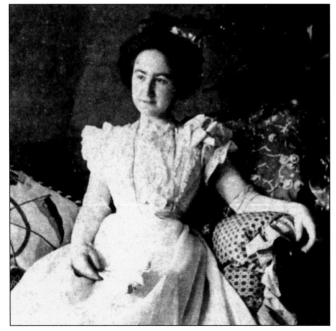

Flora Anfenger Hornbein is pictured here as a young woman at the home of her parents before her marriage to Philip Hornbein.

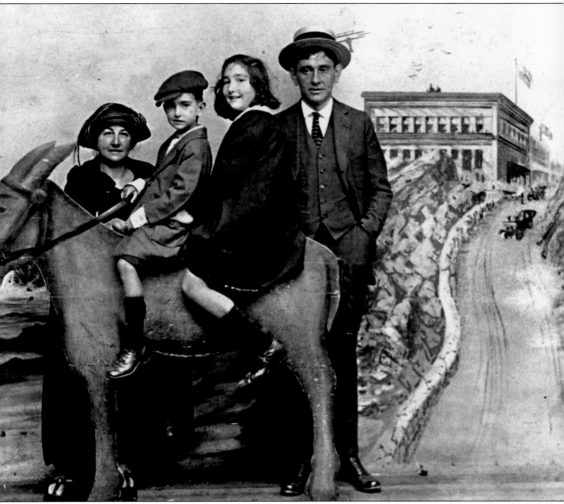

Taken on a trip to San Francisco in 1925, this photograph of the Hornbein family includes (from left to right) Flora; her son Philip Jr., who became a prominent labor attorney; her daughter Marjorie, who became a noted historian and accomplished pianist active in Jewish communal and Denver civic affairs; and her husband, Philip Sr.

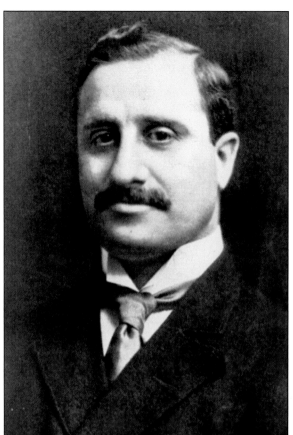

Leadville, Colorado, was the birthplace of one of the greatest family fortunes in American history. Meyer Guggenheim, the patriarch of the family, purchased a half interest in two lead and silver mines for $5,000, and by 1890, his investment was valued at $15 million. Meyer's son Simon Guggenheim, pictured here, lived in Denver and served as the only Jewish U.S. Senator from Colorado from 1907 to 1913. He was a major supporter of Denver's National Jewish Hospital. (Courtesy of the Denver Public Library, Western History Collection.)

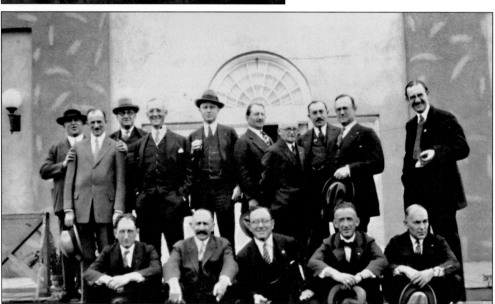

This c. 1925 photograph depicts members of the luncheon group of the Progress Club at Colfax Avenue and Williams Street. The Progress Club was founded in 1885 and was the meeting place for Denver's elite, some of whom were descendants of Denver's early Jewish pioneers.

Two

MAKING A LIVING

Although the Jewish pioneers who settled in Colorado were a small group, they took a highly active role in the economic development of the state. Some of the early 1859ers were miners and professionals; however, most were merchants who filled the role of provisioners serving the new settlements and mining communities. They established stores and businesses in the two rival camps at Cherry Creek—Auraria and Denver—and in Leadville, Central City, and Trinidad. Julius Mitchell, the eldest among the Jews in the Denver community, owned a modest grocery store later named the Bee Hive where eggs first sold for $2 a dozen, while Fred Z. Salomon managed the first general mercantile house in Colorado.

This predominantly German Jewish group of pioneers from Central Europe was later joined after 1880 by an increasing number of East European immigrants who had begun arriving in the United States in large groups following the Russian pogroms and increasing economic restrictions and religious persecution in their homeland. Significant numbers of Jews from both groups established businesses in Denver and all over the state, providing food, clothing, and services to growing populations in the burgeoning area. Such well-known companies as Guldman's Golden Eagle department store and the May Company dry goods establishment had their origins in Leadville. As Denver matured and became a large urban center, Jewish businessmen and occasionally businesswomen continued to play an important part in the city's growth and founded companies that would become national in scope, including the Shwayder Brothers Trunk Company that later evolved into the world-famous Samsonite Corporation.

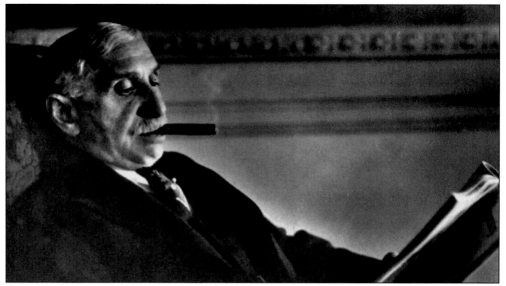

Leopold Guldman was one of Colorado's pioneer philanthropists. Born in Bavaria, he came to Colorado in 1870 in search of silver but found it more profitable to open the Golden Eagle clothing stores in Leadville and Cripple Creek. In 1879, Guldman moved to Denver and opened the third and most successful Golden Eagle enterprise. For many years, it was Denver's leading, popular-price department store. Guldman's philanthropy contributed to the growth of National Jewish Hospital, the JCRS, Beth Israel Hospital, and the Guldman Community Center, which later evolved into Denver's Jewish Community Center.

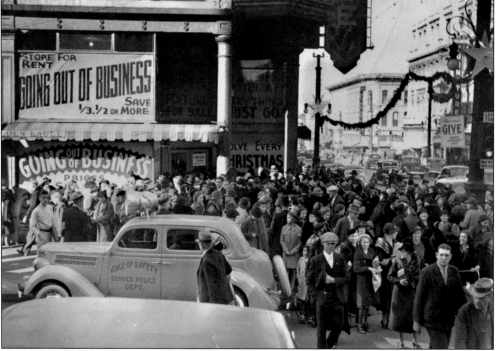

After Leopold Guldman's death in 1936, his store endured hard times and was ultimately forced to close. The last day of the Denver Golden Eagle in 1941 is pictured here.

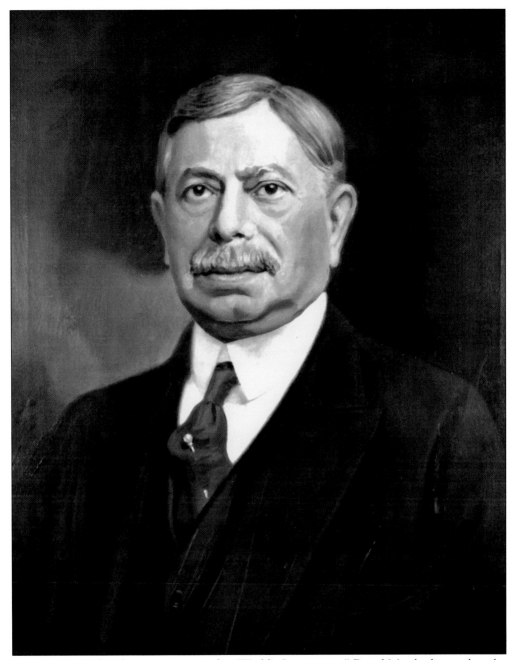

Attracted by Colorado's reputation as the "World's Sanatorium," David May had moved to the state for his health, but like so many Jewish immigrants, he found prosperity as well. Born in Bavaria, May opened his first clothing store in Leadville in 1887 where he and his partners sold Levis and long, red, woolen underwear.

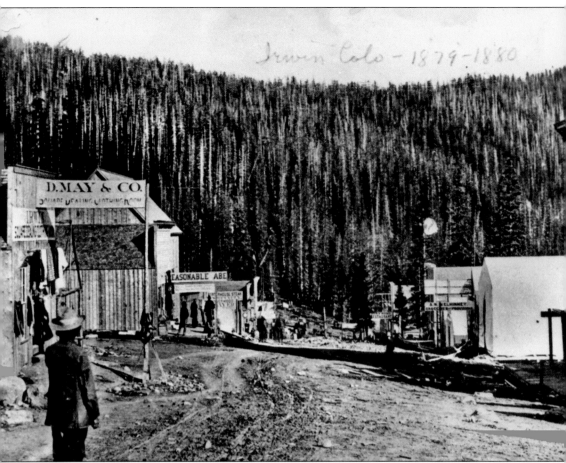

Soon David May opened branches of his store in Irwin (pictured above), Central City, and Denver. May was an active supporter of National Jewish Hospital and Temple Emanuel. The May Company evolved into one of the largest department store chains in the country.

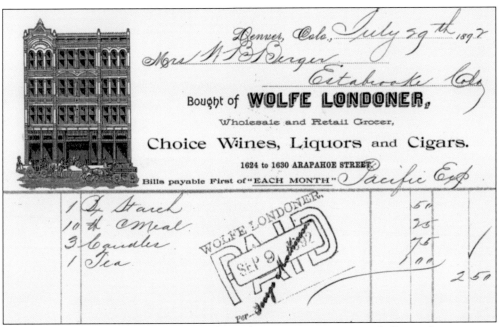

In addition to being active in politics, Wolfe Londoner was a prominent early Denver businessman. Pictured is a receipt from Wolfe Londoner Wholesale and Retail Grocer, Denver, July 29, 1892. Londoner took office as mayor of Denver on April 2, 1889.

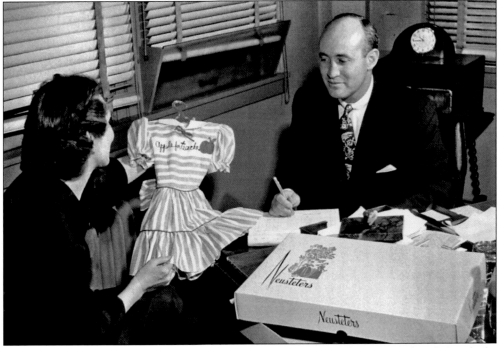

Max and Ed Neusteter were two prominent Jewish businessmen who migrated to Colorado for health reasons. They first settled in Estes Park, but by 1911, the two moved to Denver and founded the Neusteter's high fashion women's clothing store, a downtown Denver feature for many decades. Pictured here is Meyer's son Myron Neusteter, who took over the store in 1948.

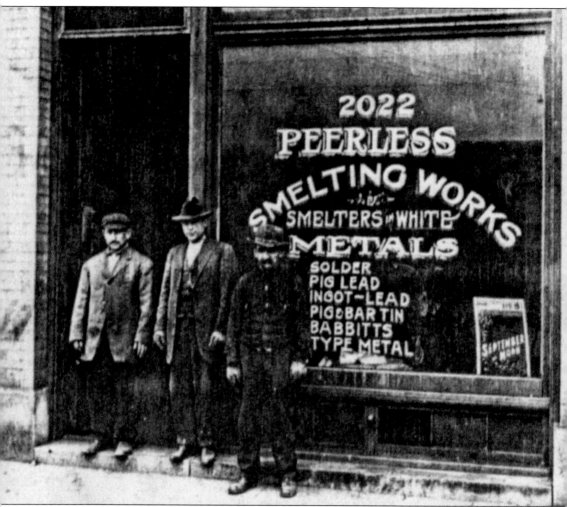

East European immigrant Adolph Kiesler began as a peddler and junk dealer. He saved enough money from odd jobs to launch the successful Peerless Alloy Company in 1908. Pictured here is Kiesler (center) in front of the Peerless Smelting Works c. 1908. Operating under the motto "Money is made to give away," Kiesler became a major philanthropist in the community.

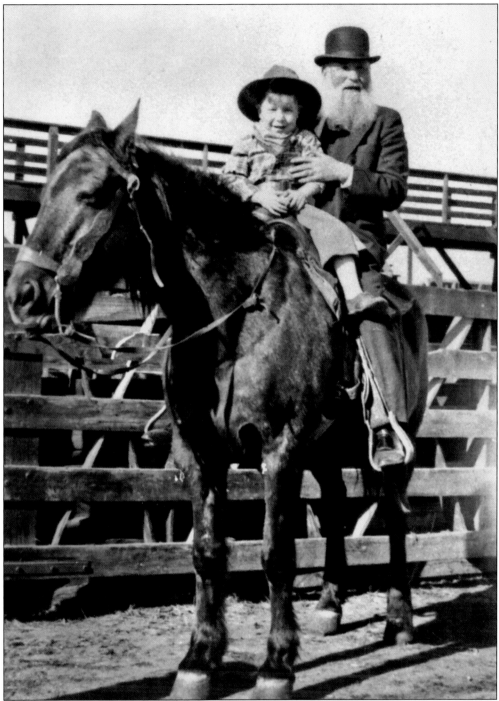

Robert Lazar Miller is pictured on horseback at the Denver Stockyards with his grandson Stanley Stein in 1932. Miller arrived in Colorado from Lithuania in 1881 and developed a ranching and meat business with his brother Joseph Miller. He became chief buyer for the K and B Packing Company and was a fixture on horseback at the Denver Stockyards until he died at the age of 96 in 1940.

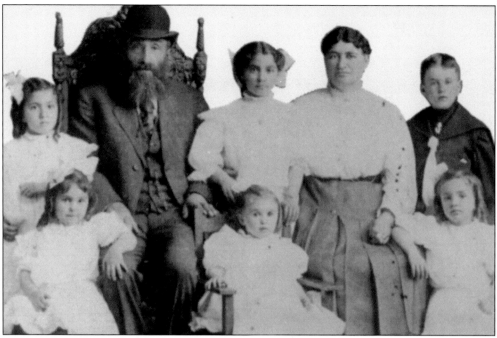

Louis Robinson established the first Robinson dairy farm in 1885. He was a vital force in developing the JCRS and donated the land on which the JCRS poultry and dairy farm were developed. Robinson Dairy remained a family enterprise for five generations. He is seated here surrounded by his family c. 1907.

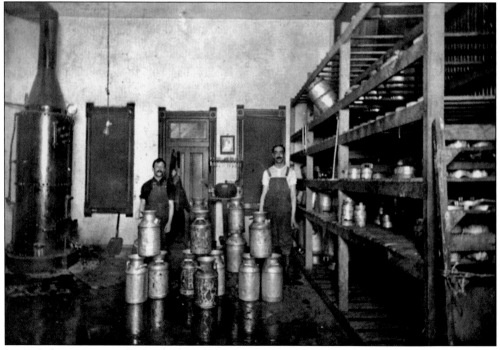

Louis Robinson's sons also worked in the business. His son Morris Robinson (right) is pictured here at the Robinson Farm Climax Dairy c. 1906.

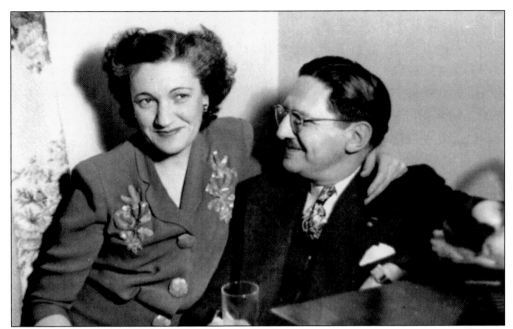

In 1927, Morris Robinson's daughter Dorothy Robinson Atler married rising Denver attorney Noah Atler, who had started his law firm in the 1920s. Noah Atler was active in many Denver Jewish and civic organizations, including the Allied Jewish Federation, B'nai B'rith, the JCRS, Big Brothers, and Kiwanis. This photograph of the Atlers was taken in 1941.

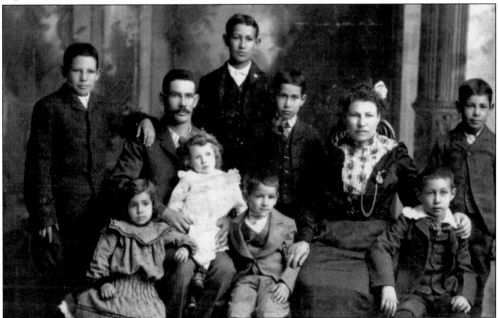

This portrait of the Abraham and Fanny Baer Judelovitz (Judd) family was taken in 1903. The Judelovitz family arrived in Denver in 1888 from Latvia, and Abraham Judelovitz became a well-known builder, contractor, and developer. He was instrumental in the construction of the Beth Ha Medrosh Hagodol (BMH) Synagogue on Gaylord Street and the Mayflower Hotel, among many other Denver buildings. For many years, he volunteered his expertise on behalf of the JCRS.

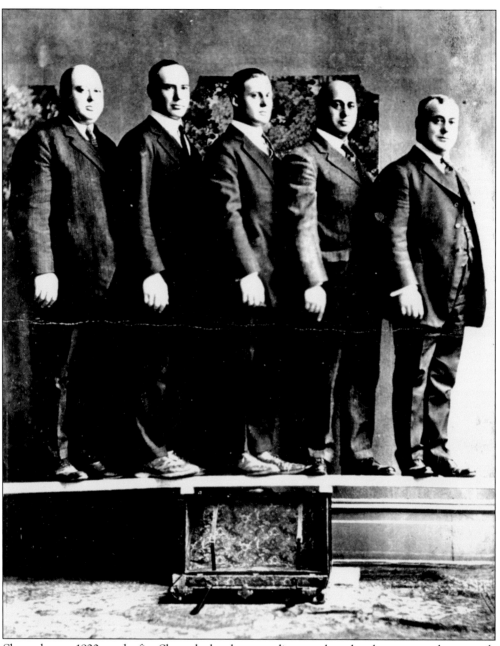

Shown here *c.* 1920 are the five Shwayder brothers standing on a board to demonstrate the strength of their suitcase. In the early 1900s, Jesse Shwayder opened a small luggage factory in Denver with his father, Isaac, and brothers Mark, Maurice, Benjamin, and Solomon. Together they eventually turned it into one of the largest luggage producers in America, the Samsonite Corporation.

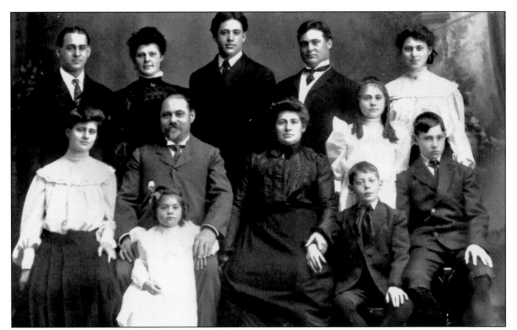

This portrait of Isaac and Rachel Kobey Shwayder and their children in Denver was taken c. 1905.

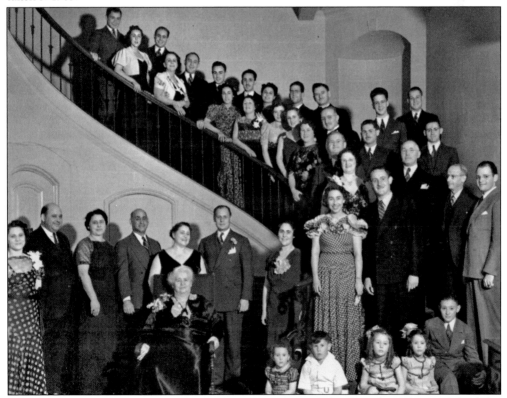

The extended Shwayder family is shown here in 1938 at Rachel Kobey Shwayder's 80th birthday celebration in Denver.

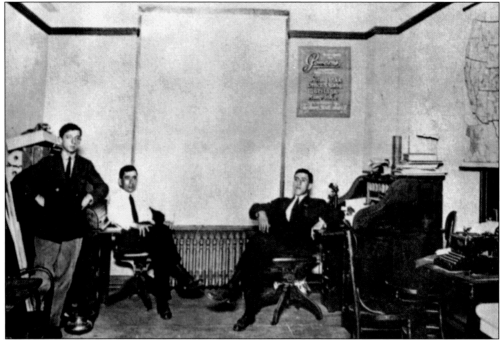

In 1906, Lulu and Henry Frankel Sr. opened Frankel Stationery at Sixteenth Street at Larimer Street. Frankel served as president of Congregation Emanuel from 1888 to 1923. Their son Henry Frankel Jr. took over the business in 1914 at the age of 22, and he guided its transformation into the Frankel Manufacturing Company, which produced typewriter ribbons as its first product. It became one of the largest firms of its kind in the world. Pictured here is the early Frankel Stationery Retail Office in 1910 with Henry Jr. seated, right.

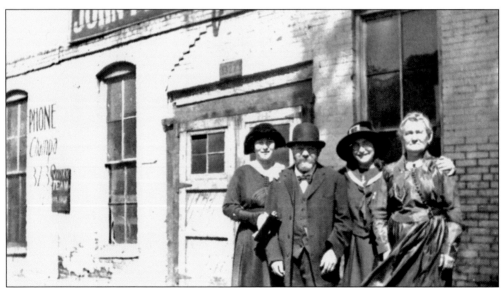

Polish-born Abraham Isaacs started life in Colorado in Leadville but moved his blacksmith shop to Denver in the first decade of the 20th century. He is shown here in front of his shop with his wife and granddaughters c. 1914.

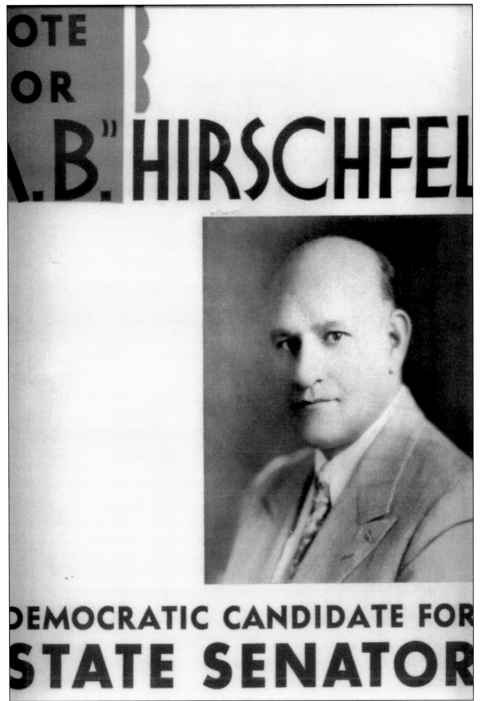

Born in 1888 in Cincinnati to Russian Jewish parents, Abraham Bernard Hirschfeld took his passion for printing and a small, $35 handpress and turned it into the largest printing business in the Rocky Mountain region in 1907. A. B., as he was known, was active in Jewish communal and Denver civic affairs. In 1935, he was elected to serve as a Colorado state senator, a position he held until 1941. He is shown here in an election poster.

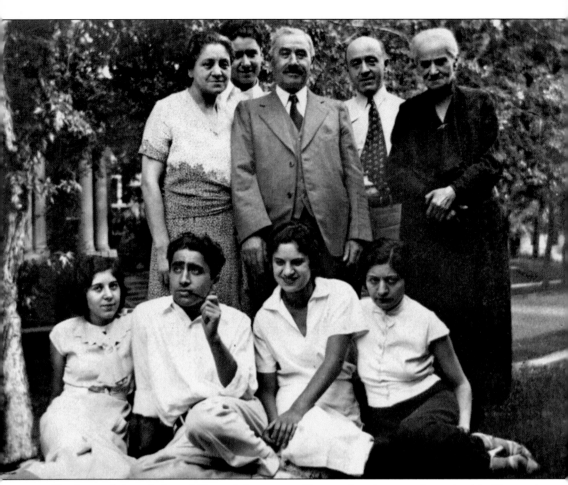

Brother and sister Jack and Hannah Levy were German immigrants who arrived in Denver in the 1920s and soon became leading Colorado entrepreneurs. They opened the Hosiery Bar, and by 1936, the Levys were running five Fashion Bar stores, two in Denver, one in Colorado Springs, and one each in Pueblo and Greeley. Pictured are members of the Hilb and Levy families in Denver c. 1930. From left to right are (first row) Ruth Levy Wohlauer, Edward Levy, Kate Levy Zigmond, and Hannah Levy; (second row) Bertha Levy, Jack Levy, Raphael Levy, Isidore Hilb, and Mina Hilb.

The Levy family supported numerous community institutions, including Rose Hospital and the University of Denver. Hannah Levy, pictured here as a young woman, used her interest in fashion to serve as chief buyer for the Fashion Bar stores.

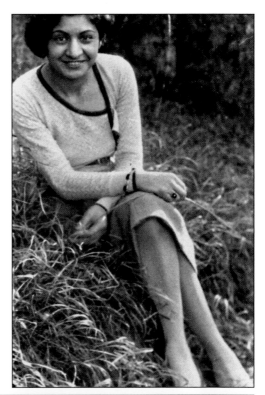

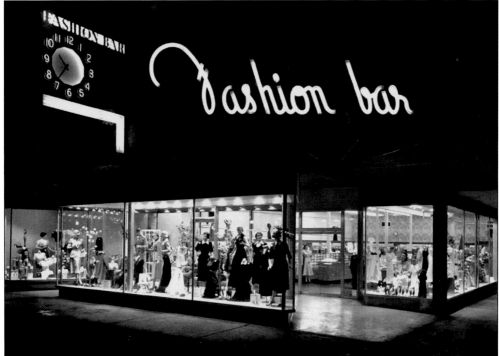

Shown here is a typical Fashion Bar window display. By the 1980s, Fashion Bar employed more than 1,700 people in 80 stores spread out throughout the West.

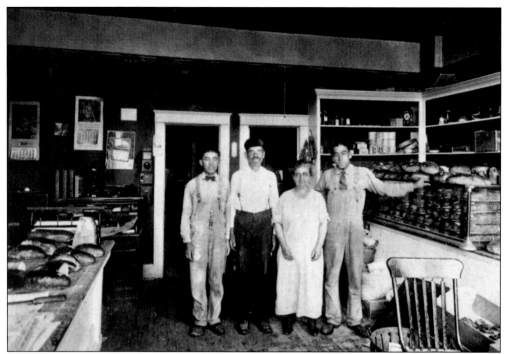

Many early Jewish Denver residents opened grocery stores or food establishments. Star Bakery was founded by East European immigrants Eva and Jacob Boscowitz in 1907. Pictured from left to right are Rudy Boscowitz (Boscoe), Elya Rubin, Eva Boscowitz, Sam Boscowitz (Boscoe).

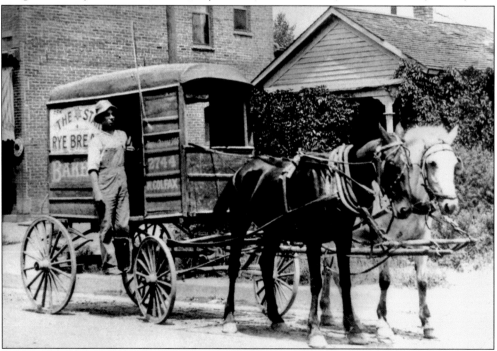

The Star Bakery delivery truck, shown here c. 1915, was a familiar sight on Denver west-side streets and throughout the city for many years.

Jewish women often helped support their families by operating their own stores. Annie Orlinsky Miller and daughters Sara and Celia appear here in front of Orlinsky's Grocery c. 1910.

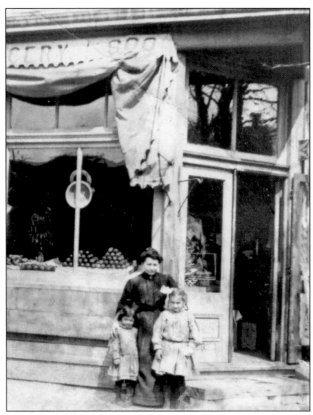

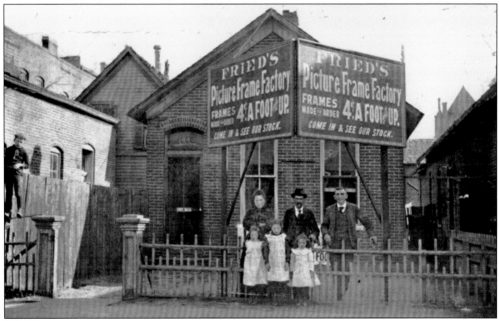

Pictured here are members of the Fried family standing in front of the Fried's Picture Frame Factory in Denver c. 1910. Kate, Bela, and Eugene Fried stand behind an iron fence; Kate's three daughters, Bertha, Mary, and Sally, stand in front of the fence.

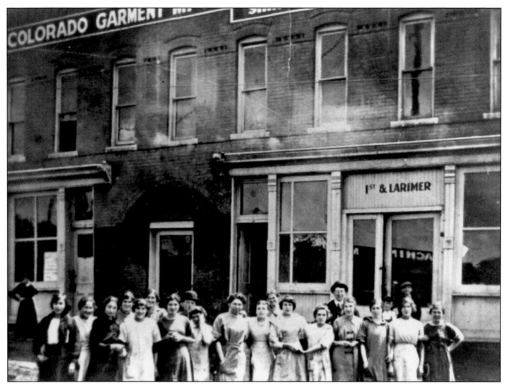

The Lutz family operated the Colorado Garment Manufacturing Company, which produced shirts and overalls, on Denver's Larimer Street. The factory employed many immigrant Jewish women in the early years of the 20th century, as shown here c. 1910. Leon Obodov, shown eighth from left, served as the manager of the company from 1905 to 1910.

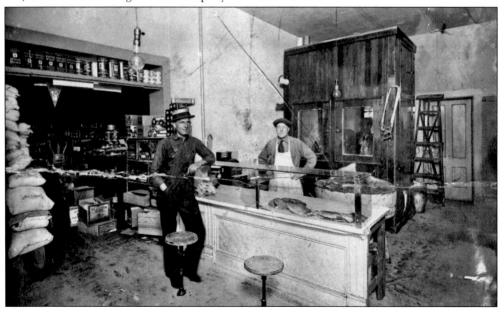

Many Jewish businessmen started establishments to serve the Jewish kosher trade. Phil Brown is pictured here in his kosher butcher shop in 1921.

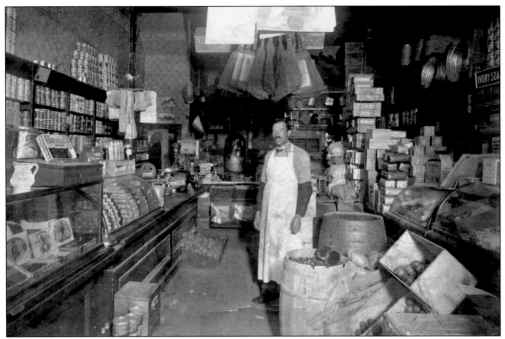

Morris Eber appears here behind the counter of Eber's Grocery, located at 1463 Platte Street in Denver in 1912.

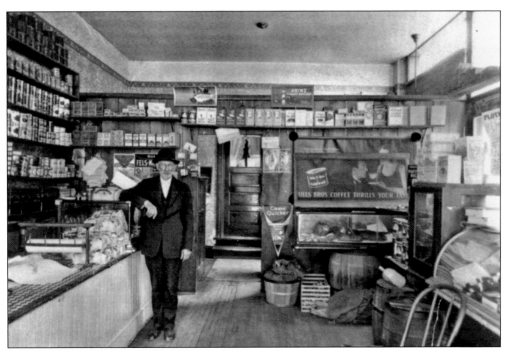

Label Ginsburg is shown standing in his grocery store, located on Grove Street in Denver's west-side Colfax Jewish community c. 1925. When a sign painter made a mistake and spelled the Ginsberg surname with a "u" instead of an "e," Label changed the family name to Ginsburg.

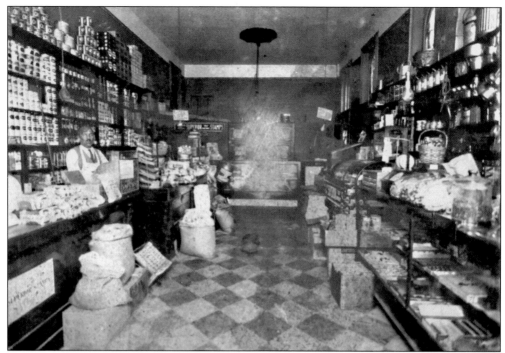

Abraham Cwengel is shown here at the cash register at Cwengel's Grocery Store on Larimer Street in Denver *c.* 1930.

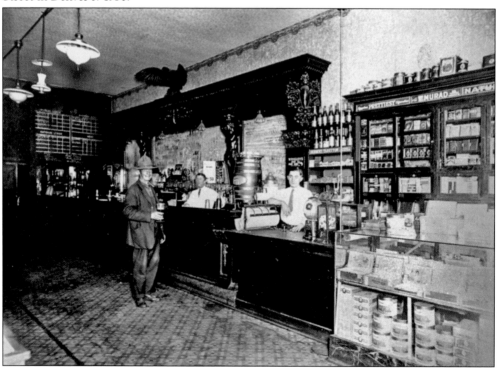

Saliman's restaurant was a popular downtown Denver establishment and was located on Larimer Street. It is shown here in the 1920s.

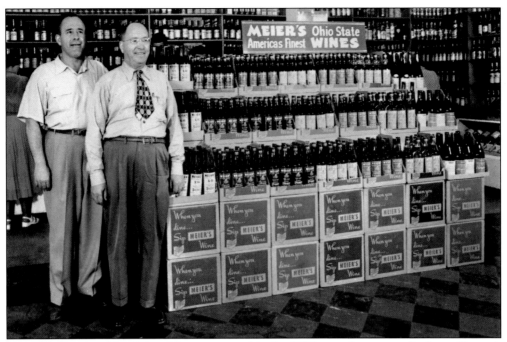

Harry Hoffman and his father, Morris, pictured in the 1950s, stand next to a display at Denver's landmark Hoffman Liquor Store. The liquor establishment was founded in 1937.

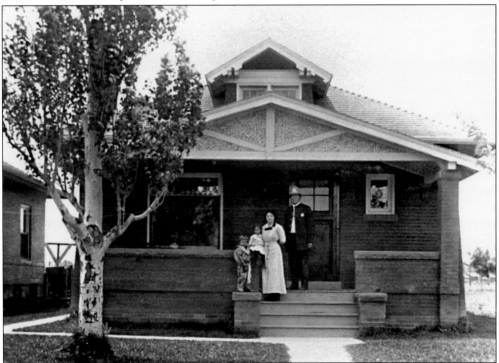

William Goldblatt followed an unusual profession for a Denver Jewish citizen when he became a local fireman. He is pictured here in uniform with his wife, Helen, and children Ruth and Marvin on the porch of their Newton Street house in Denver in 1914.

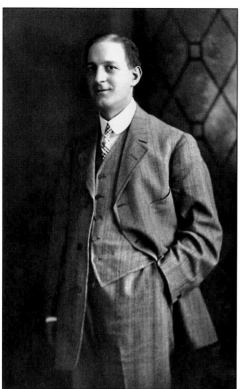

Medicine was a popular profession among Denver's Jews. Dr. Saling Simon, pictured here as a young man, was born in New York City, but after graduating from college, he developed tuberculosis and migrated to Denver in search of a cure. Saling went on to receive a medical degree from Denver's Gross Medical College in 1895 and stayed to treat other tuberculosis victims, opening his practice in the same year. He was a member of Temple Emanuel and president of the local B'nai B'rith in 1896. From 1917 to 1919, he served as medical director of National Jewish Hospital, where he instituted the research department.

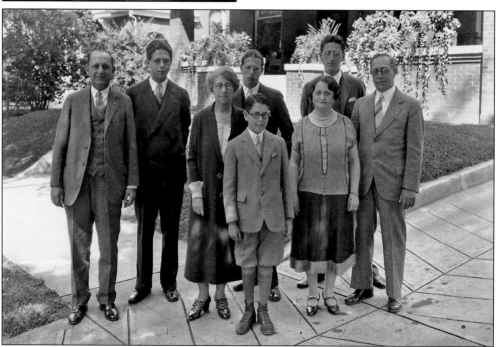

In this 1926 photograph taken in front of the Simon home at 1316 Gilpin Street, Dr. Saling Simon (left) is pictured with his wife, Sarah, and four sons Herb, Walter, Richard, and Edward (front), and his sister and brother-in-law Eva and Sam Kreisman.

Dr. Emanuel Friedman, pictured here as a young man, also came to Colorado because of tuberculosis. After recovering his health, he opened his office on West Colfax Avenue in the immigrant community and was one of Denver's first pediatricians. He graduated from Denver's Gross Medical College in 1904 and also served on the medical staff at National Jewish Hospital and the JCRS.

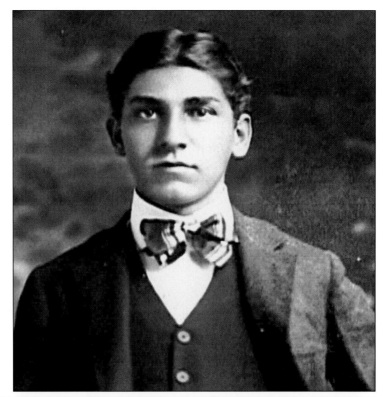

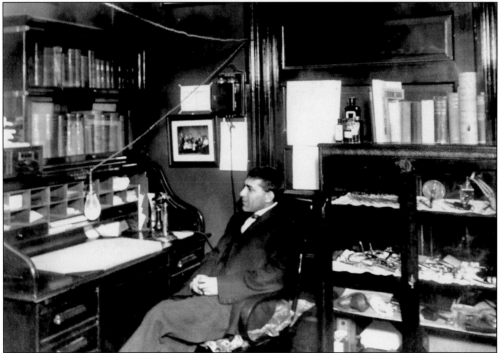

Dr. Emanuel Friedman is seated at his office desk in 1908. He was still making house calls to visit his patients the evening before he died.

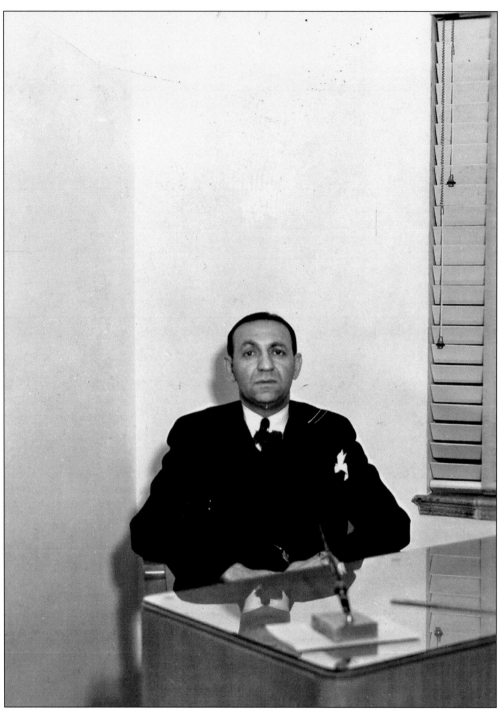

Dr. Arthur Esserman, seated at the desk of his children's clinic, began his career in partnership with Dr. Emanuel Friedman. Esserman was an intern at the Children's Hospital in Denver from 1924 to 1926. He was later on the staff of the hospital and practiced pediatric medicine in Denver from 1926 until his untimely death in 1952.

Denver Jewish businessmen opened a variety of stores to serve the community. Harry Gordon migrated from Lithuania to New York before settling in Denver, where he founded the Gordon Sign Company, shown here c. 1905. He married Esther Nissenbaum in Denver on June 4, 1911.

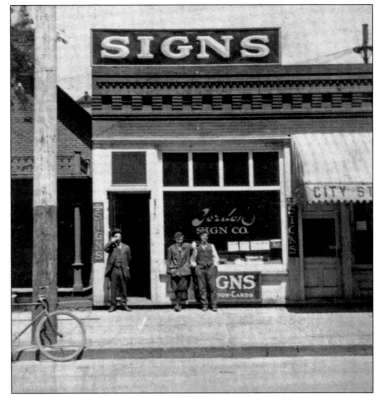

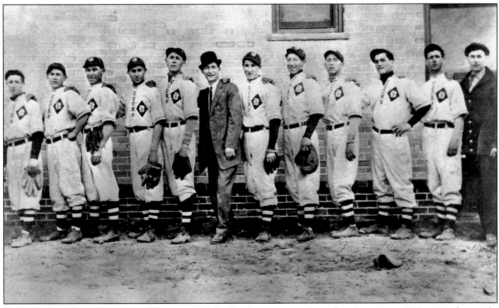

Russian Jewish immigrants Harry and Ida Cook journeyed to the American West in the early 1890s. They later opened Cook's Russian Baths in Denver. It served both as a *mikvah* (ritual bath) operated at night for women by Ida and during the day as a popular steam bath open to the public, complete with catered kosher meals. Pictured here c. 1918 is the business's baseball team with Sammy Kantrowitz, its coach.

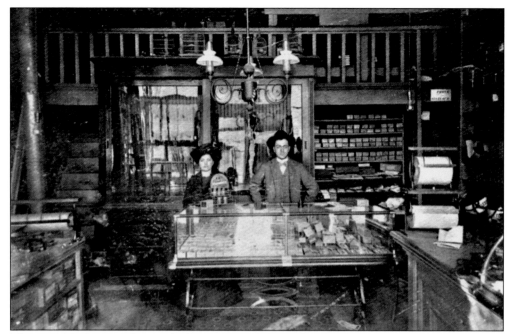

The *c.* 1900 photograph reveals the interior of the Colorado Electric Wiring Company with proprietor Benjamin Borwick standing with his sister Bessie.

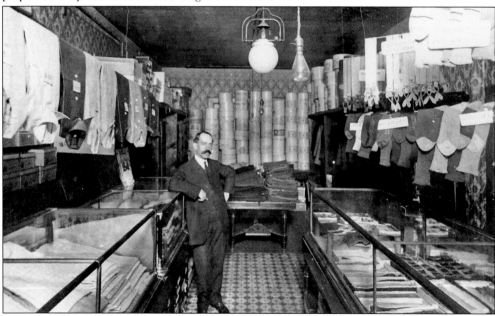

Abraham Grossman appears here in his store, the Grossman's Haberdashery, in Denver around 1920. The store was located on Sixteenth Street, Denver's main downtown business thoroughfare. He originally immigrated to America from the Austro-Hungarian Empire and moved to Denver because of tuberculosis in the family. Grossman was an active member of the traditional Beth Ha Medrosh Hagodol (BMH) Synagogue and later of the Oheb Zedek Congregation, which broke away from BMH in 1911. The Oheb Zedek Congregation rejoined the parent synagogue toward the end of the Great Depression.

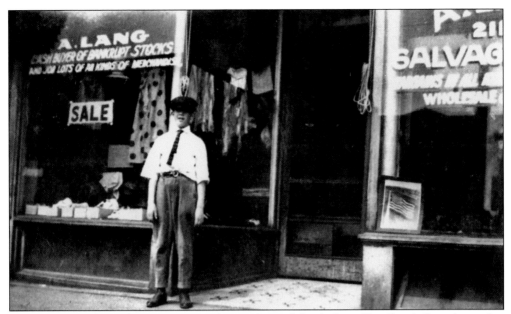

Arthur Lang is shown here c. 1919 standing in front of the A. Lang Dry Goods Store located at 2115 Larimer Street in Denver.

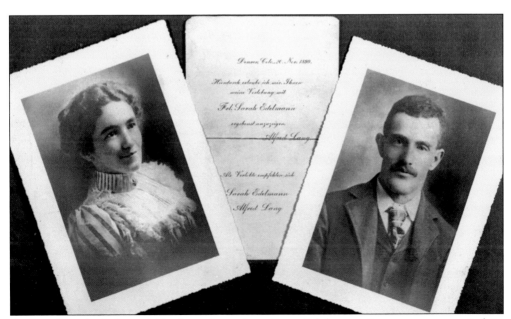

Arthur Lang's father, Alfred, and mother, Sara Edelmann Lang, were married in Denver in 1900.

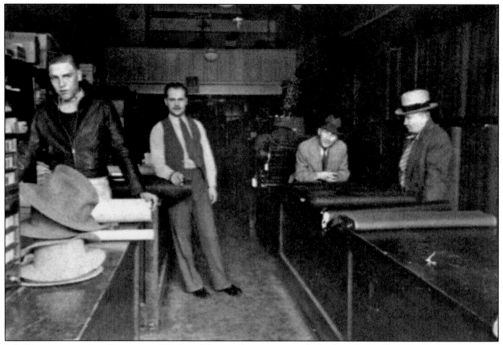

I. J. Shore arrived in Denver in 1920 and began his career with his brother selling tailor's trimmings and woolens. In this 1935 picture, I. J. Shore (center) is standing in the store of M. Shore and Sons in Denver.

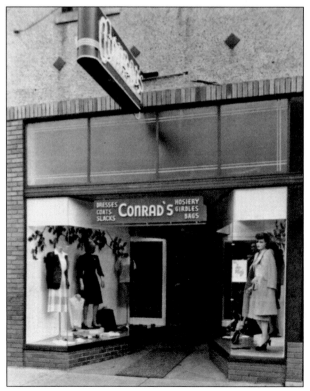

I. J. Shore later went into the wholesale ladies coat and dress business before developing Conrad's Mademoiselle Shops, which were organized in 1938. The business was a successful chain of 30 ready-to-wear women's clothing shops. Pictured here is a Conrad store in the 1950s.

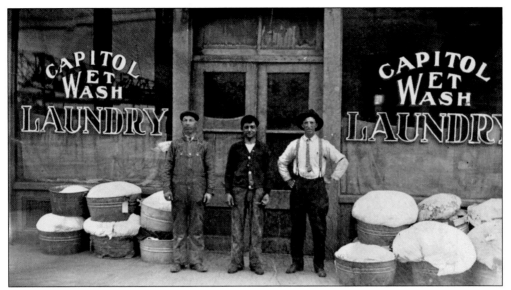

The Capitol Wet Wash Laundry was located at 2700 West Colfax Avenue. Owner Joe Sosne (right) is pictured with his employees in about 1915.

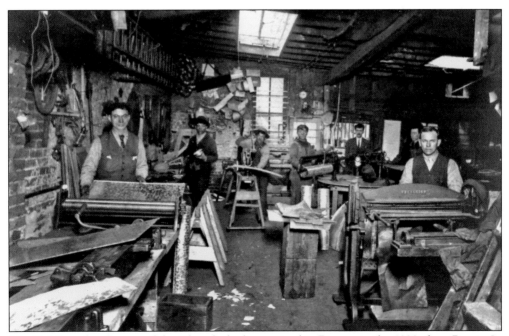

The Goldberg family, part of the Glazerlach clan, arrived in Denver in the 1890s from Russia. In the early 1900s, Louis and Nathan Goldberg opened a tin shop. They were later joined by their younger brothers William and Jacob Goldberg, and eventually went into the film equipment business. Pictured here is the interior of Goldberg Brothers Tinners in the 1930s.

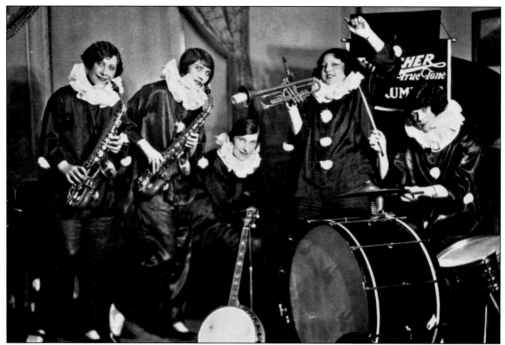

Dressed in clown costumes, Billie Stein (with trumpet) and her band members appeared in Denver in 1925.

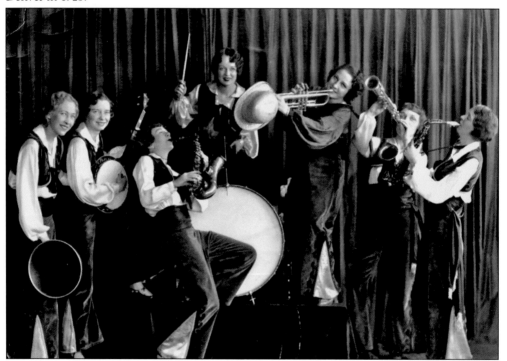

Billie (Lillian) Stein started her own all-girls band at the age of 14 and traveled throughout the United States performing on her trumpet. Billie is pictured here *c.* 1930, trumpet in hand, with her Harmony Girls Band in Denver.

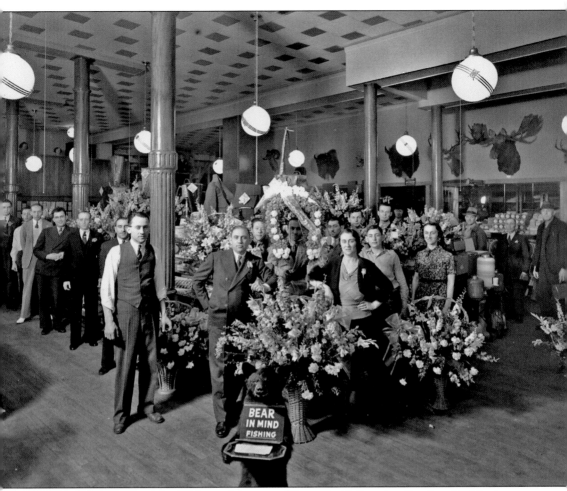

This photograph captured the 1936 grand opening of Dave Cook's Sporting Goods at 1601 Larimer Street. Pictured from left to right are Jack Bernstone, Dave Cook, Jane Cook, Herb Cook, and Belle Smernoff. In 1924, Dave and Max Cook went into the sporting goods business, operating the first major sports store in Colorado. Dave bought out his brother's share in the business in 1932 and became well known as a pioneering innovator in the field.

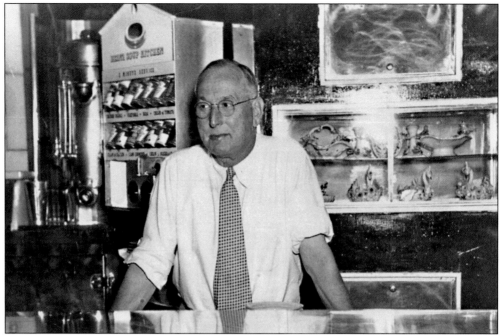

Azriel Stein's Pencol Drug Store was a fixture on the Denver landscape for many decades. In addition to dispensing prescriptions, Pencol Drugs featured a popular soda and ice cream fountain and a gift section. Here Azriel Stein, a successful pharmacist and businessman, stands in front of his sales counter at Pencol Drugs. Azriel was married to Irene Stein, a noted Denver artist and daughter of Denver pioneer Robert Lazar Miller.

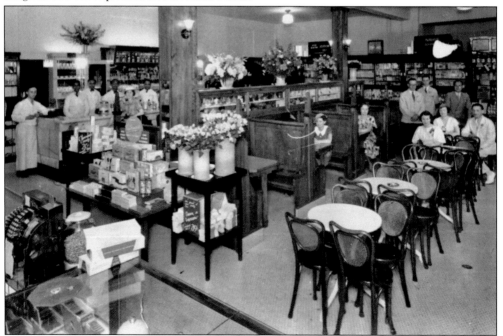

The interior of Pencol Drugs, located at Pennsylvania Street and Colfax Avenue in Denver, is shown here in the 1940s. It included a refreshment area and shelves filled with inviting gift choices.

Three

ESTABLISHING
JEWISH LIFE

Services for *Rosh Hashonah*, the Jewish New Year, were held in that first year of the "Big Excitement" when gold was discovered in Colorado in 1859. It appears that grocer Julius Mitchell, the patriarch of the group, led the services with other early Jewish residents Leopold Mayer, Abraham Jacobs, and Fred Z. Salomon, among others, in attendance. Although the early Jewish pioneers in Denver identified with their fellow Jews, most of their energies were directed toward establishing a foothold in the burgeoning frontier town, and many became leaders in the city's political, social, and economic life. However, a Hebrew Burial and Prayer Society, also known as the Hebrew Cemetery Association, was formed as early as 1860. It was Denver's first known Jewish organization.

By 1870, these men and women, largely of German Jewish extraction, had more time to confront the task of building an organized Jewish community. In 1871, a Hebrew Benevolent Society and a Ladies' Hebrew Benevolent Society were formed, followed by the establishment of the Denver chapter of the national fraternal order B'nai B'rith in 1872 and the incorporation of Congregation Emanuel in 1874. Before the turn of the 20th century, the traditional Beth Ha Medrosh Hagodol (BMH) Synagogue had emerged as a major institution as well. With the influx of East European Jews in the 1880s, many Russian Jews settled on Denver's west side, and soon numerous small shuls, kosher meat shops, and bakeries dotted the Orthodox Jewish enclave.

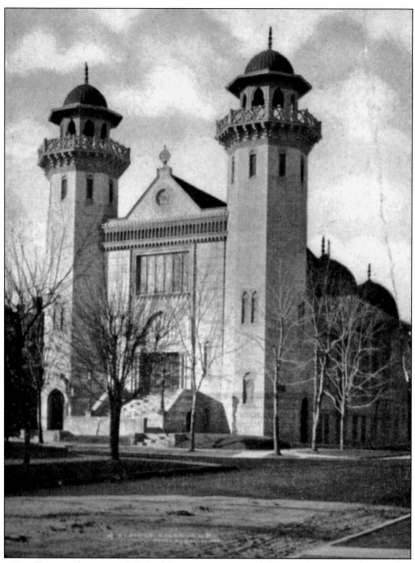

Congregation Emanuel was established in Denver in 1874. The reform temple was designed in classic Moorish style, and the impressive building, the congregation's third home, appeared here as a picture postcard in 1907.

Rabbi William Friedman became the spiritual leader of Congregation Emanuel in 1899 and served in that capacity until 1938. A graduate of Hebrew Union College and a leader in the movement of Reform Judaism, he was renowned for his classic oratory and high civic profile in Denver, and was also a founder of National Jewish Hospital and Community Chest, a nonsectarian charity organization.

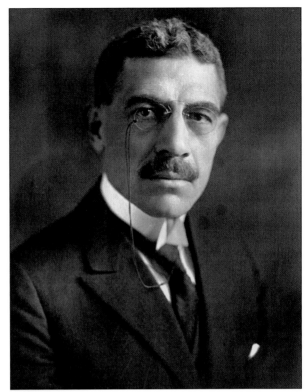

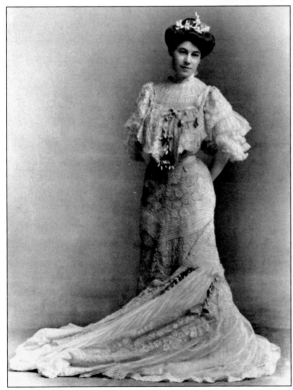

Pictured in her wedding dress in 1903 is Juliet Freyhan Friedman, wife of Rabbi William Friedman.

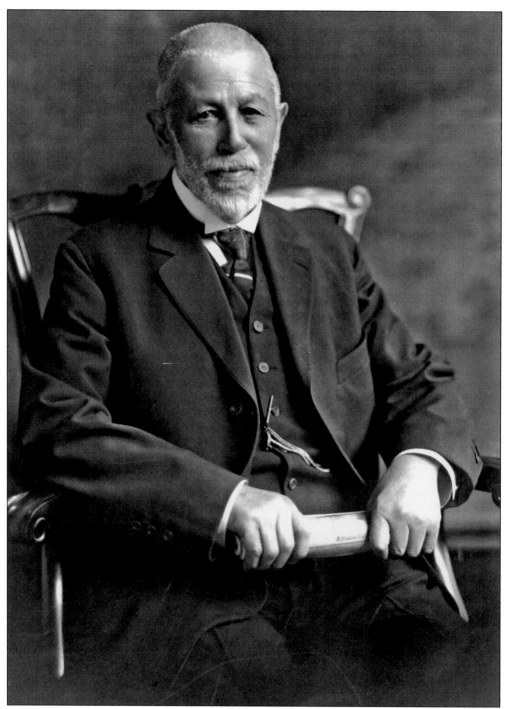

Denver's East European population began with a trickle. Polish-born Henry Plonsky was one of the earliest to arrive in 1877. He helped form an Orthodox *minyan* above his store on Larimer Street. He became a successful shoe and boot merchant in partnership with Leopold Mayer and was instrumental in the establishment of the Orthodox Jewish congregation Ahavey Emunah in 1880 and later the traditional BMH Synagogue and the Beth Joseph congregation.

Rabbi Charles Eliezar Hillel Kauvar became the first rabbi of the Beth HaMedrosh Hagodol (BMH) Synagogue in 1901 and served in that position for more than 50 years. Armed with a master's degree from Columbia University and a rabbinical degree from the traditional New York Jewish Theological Seminary, he introduced traditional Judaism within a modern American context to his congregants. Kauvar was an ardent Zionist and supporter of the JCRS.

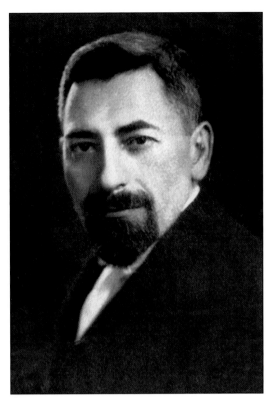

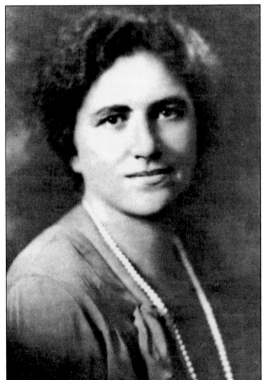

Belle Bluestone Kauvar, wife of Rabbi Kauvar, was an early leader in the Denver chapter of Hadassah, which was organized in 1915. Hadassah combined the Jewish emphasis on social welfare with the ideology of Zionism. Belle's brother Dr. Ephraim Michael Bluestone later served as the director of the Hadassah Medical Organization in Palestine between 1926 and 1928.

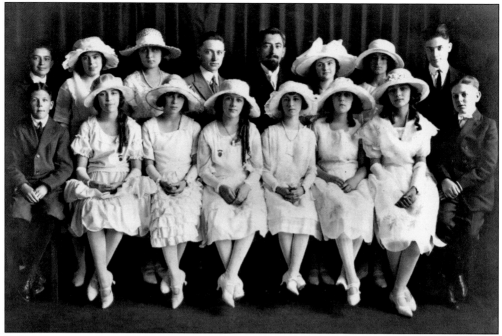

Rabbi Kauvar is pictured here with the BMH confirmation class of 1921.

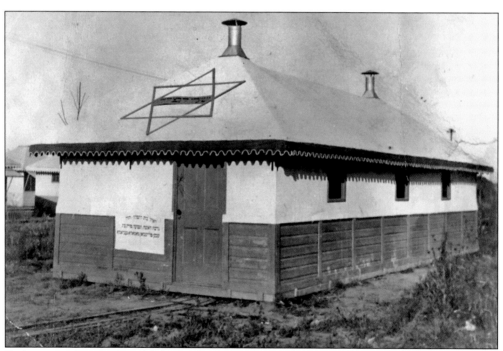

Early synagogues were established at both of Denver's Jewish tuberculosis sanatoriums. At the Jewish Consumptives' Relief Society (JCRS), this tent served as a synagogue before a permanent building could be erected in 1911.

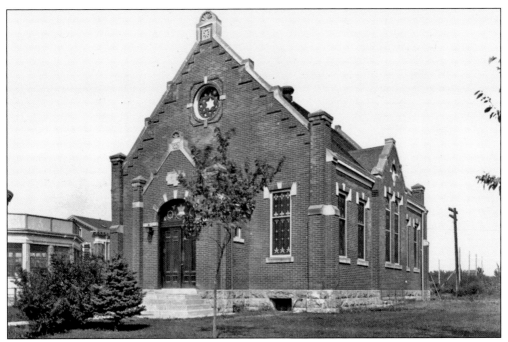

The Lewisohn Chapel at National Jewish Hospital, pictured here, was established in 1909.

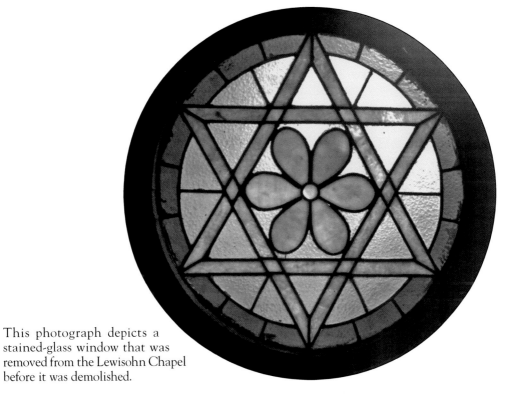

This photograph depicts a stained-glass window that was removed from the Lewisohn Chapel before it was demolished.

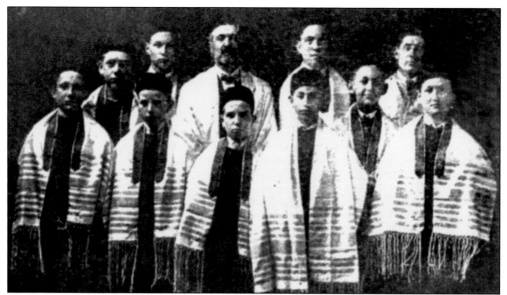

The Oheb Zedek Congregation, or the "Marion Street Shul" as it was also known, broke away from the BMH Synagogue in 1911 but reunited with it in the 1940s. Pictured here are members of the boys' choir c. 1920. Sydney Grossman, son of merchant Abraham Grossman, is pictured standing third from left. He became an attorney and a prominent leader in Denver's Jewish community as president of both the Jewish Family and Children's Service (now the Jewish Family Service of Colorado) and the BMH Synagogue.

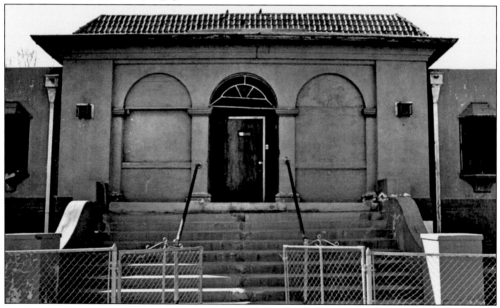

Congregation Zera Abraham was originally organized as a Chassidic Orthodox Jewish congregation in 1877, making it the oldest congregation today on the west side of Denver. The building shown here at Julian Street and West Conejos Place was the congregation's second home. It was purchased in 1938 from the Workmen's Circle, which originally erected the edifice as the Labor Lyceum, an educational center. The congregation is still active today at its third location on Winona Court. (Courtesy of Charles McNamara.)

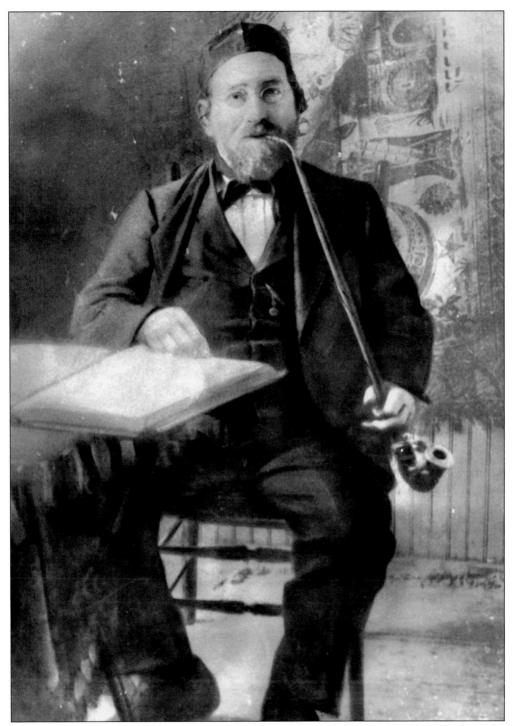

Shul Baer Milstein, pictured here, was an active leader at the early Congregation Zera Abraham. He was the patriarch of the Cotopaxi colonists, who had been involved in an ultimately unsuccessful attempt to found a Jewish agricultural colony in southern Colorado in the early 1880s. Milstein worked as a kosher butcher in Denver at the turn of the 20th century.

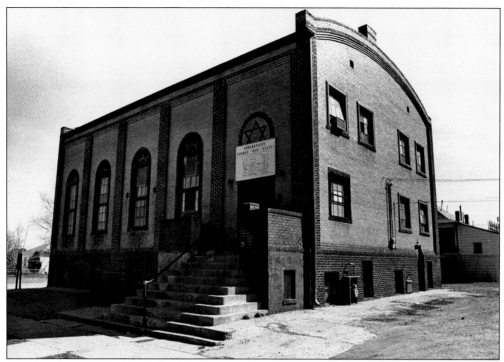

Many small synagogues, or *shuls*, sprung up in Denver's west-side East European immigrant Jewish community, including Yad Achass, more commonly known as the Rumanian shul. It was organized in 1903, and its second home, pictured here, was at the corner of King Street and Conejos Place. (Courtesy of Charles McNamara.)

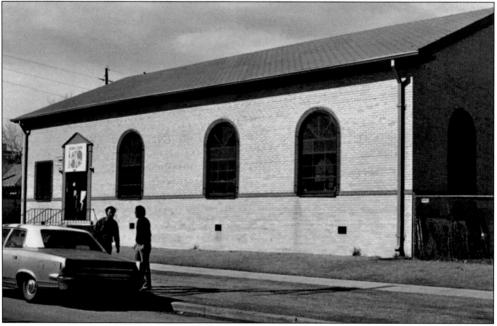

The Ostrover shul was located at Fourteenth Avenue and Lowell Boulevard. (Courtesy of Charles McNamara.)

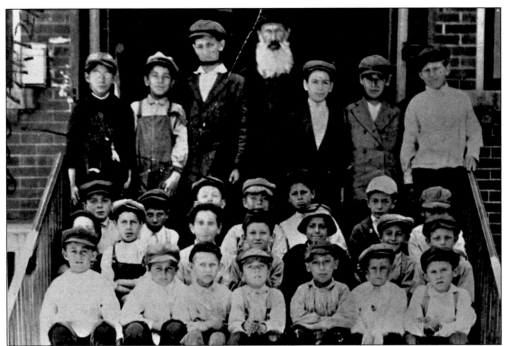

Hebrew school students are pictured here on the steps of the Yeshiva Etz Chaim building with their teacher, or *rebbe, c.* 1913. It was located at 2852 West Fourteenth Place in Denver's Jewish immigrant enclave.

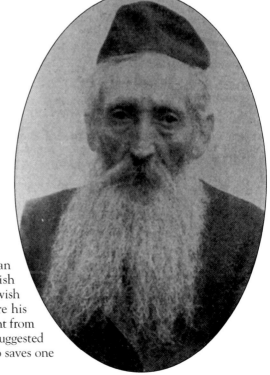

Rabbi Elias Hillkowitz was considered the dean of Denver's early west-side Orthodox Jewish rabbis. He was an early supporter of the Jewish Consumptives' Relief Society (JCRS), where his son, Dr. Philip Hillkowitz, served as president from 1904 to 1948. It was Rabbi Hillkowitz who suggested the JCRS motto from the *Talmud*: "He who saves one life saves the world."

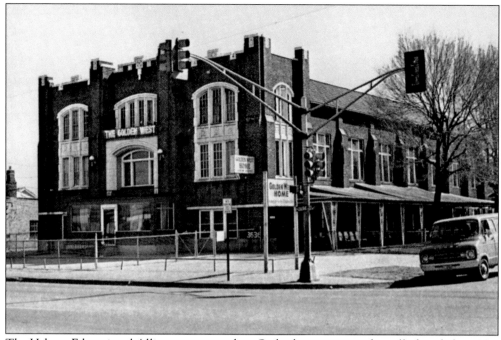

The Hebrew Educational Alliance was a modern Orthodox synagogue formally founded in 1932, and it became the largest congregation on Denver's west side.

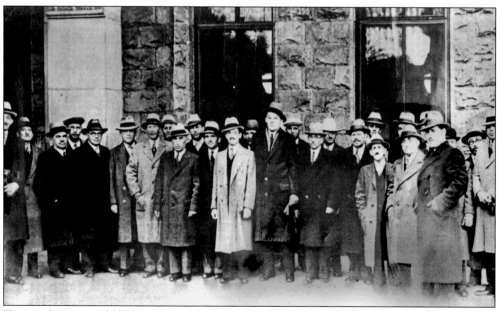

Twenty-three-year-old Rabbi Manuel Laderman (tallest man in the crowd) arrived in Denver in October 1932 to become the spiritual leader of the Hebrew Educational Alliance. He was greeted at Union Station by delegates from the synagogue.

The Orthodox Shearith Israel synagogue was established in 1899. Known as the "Tenth Street Shul," the young congregation bought this small, stone edifice from a church in 1903 and remodeled the building to suit its needs as a synagogue. Located on the outskirts of Denver's downtown area, it was convenient for Denver businessmen who were seeking a regular *minyan*. The shul was packed for daily and Sabbath services during the Great Depression because it was always well heated. (Exterior and interior photographs courtesy of Jack Goldman.)

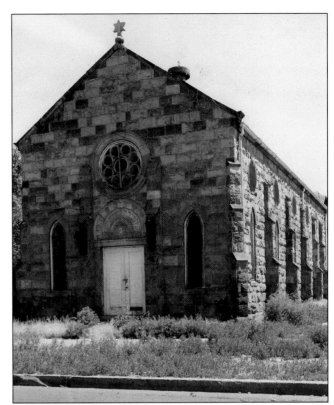

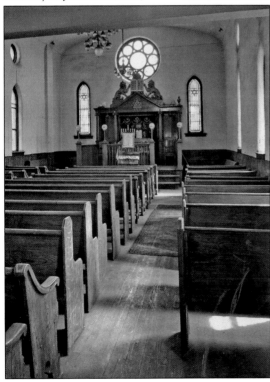

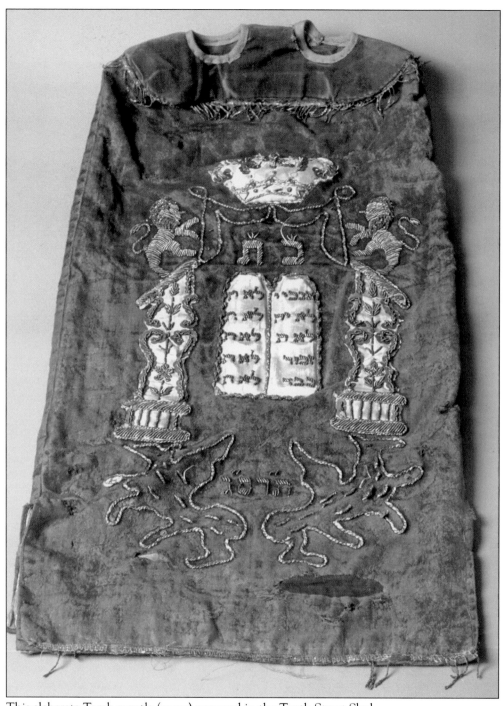

This elaborate Torah mantle (cover) was used in the Tenth Street Shul.

Four

JEWISH BENEVOLENCE

Concern and responsibility for those in need has always been a basic tenet of Jewish life, and these underlying principles informed the evolving Denver community from the beginning. The Hebrew Burial and Prayer Society, which was formed in 1860, dealt with burials, religious services for the dead, and aid and comfort for the bereaved. In 1871, the Hebrew Burial Society was reformed as the Hebrew Benevolent Society, and it joined forces with the Hebrew Ladies' Benevolent Society to carry out charity work more effectively.

Philanthropy became a particularly key focus for many Denver Jewish women as frontier life brought increased welfare demands, and they were highly visible in the public sphere in developing and sustaining Jewish and general community institutions. Frances Wisebart Jacobs, Denver's "Mother of Charities," set a standard for others to follow, and numerous philanthropic organizations were established and began to flourish around the turn of the 20th century as a new flux of predominantly East European immigrants augmented the Denver Jewish community. Most notable was the creation of two Jewish sanatoriums for tuberculosis care, the National Jewish Hospital for Consumptives (NJH), which opened in 1899, and the Jewish Consumptives' Relief Society (JCRS), which followed in 1904. Both were formally nonsectarian, although the vast majority of patients in both institutions for many years were immigrant Jews, and both offered their services free of charge to all patients, the only sanatoriums in Colorado to do so. Children in need found a haven in the Jewish Sheltering Home, which opened in 1907, and by 1917, plans were being finalized for the creation of the Beth Israel Hospital and Home for the Elderly.

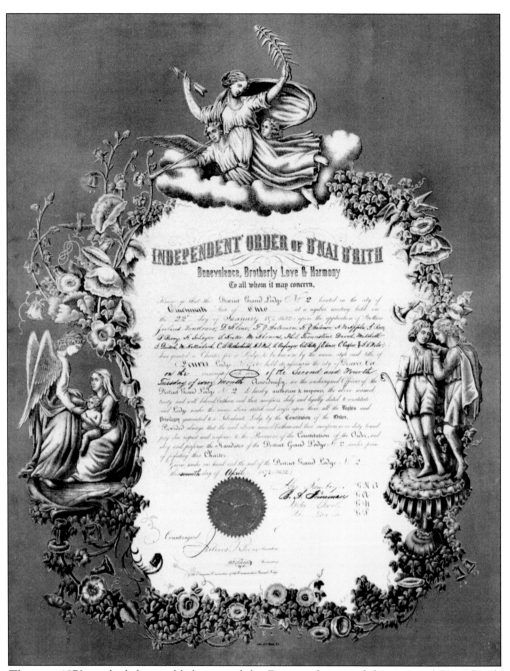

The year 1872 marked the establishment of the Denver chapter of the national B'nai B'rith organization, a social and philanthropic organization for men dedicated to humanitarian causes, science, and the arts. Pictured here is the original Denver charter dated April 7, 1872. A number of Denver's early prominent Jewish pioneers are listed on the charter, including Julius Londoner, David Kline, Fred Z. Salomon and his brother Hyman, Michael Hattenbach, Louis Anfenger, Philip Trounstine, Edward Pisko, and Dr. John Elsner.

Denver Jewish pioneer merchant David Kline, who moved to the city in 1865, served as the first president of Denver's B'nai B'rith Lodge No. 171. He and Charles Schayer had also been leading members of the Hebrew Burial Society, which evolved into the Hebrew Benevolent Society.

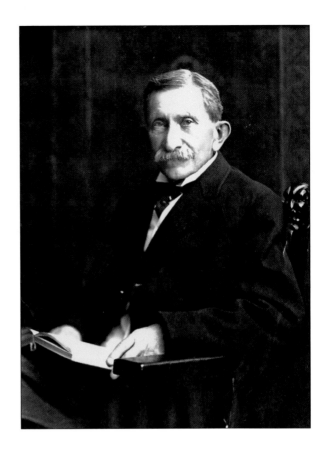

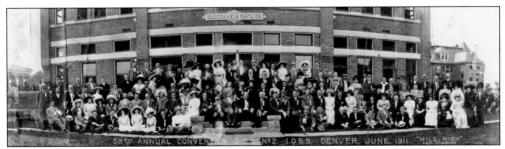

This photograph shows delegates to the 59th Annual Convention of the International Order of B'nai B'rith posed in front of the Guggenheim Pavilion at National Jewish Hospital. The convention was held in Denver in June 1911.

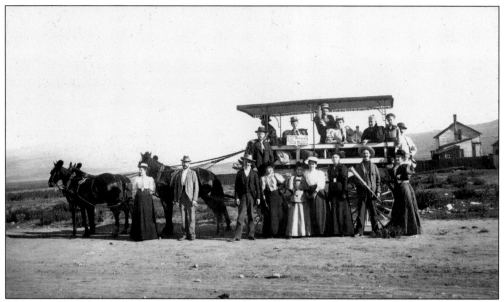

The Denver section of the National Council of Jewish Women (NCJW) was founded in 1893, the same year the national organization was established to promote Jewish education, philanthropy, and social reform. The early group of women worked to offer aid and to Americanize East European immigrants at the turn of the 20th century. This photograph depicts a horse-drawn wagon advertising a kosher picnic held at Twin Lakes in Leadville, Colorado, sponsored by the local Denver organization in 1895.

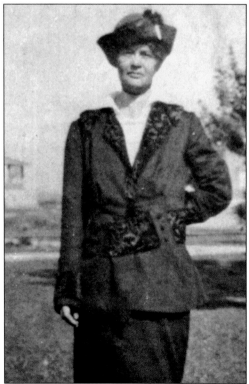

Ray David served as the hired superintendent of Denver's early Jewish Aid Society to supervise relief activities. She was nicknamed "Little Mother to the Poor" for her settlement work with East European Jewish immigrants. A leading figure in Denver society, Ray David was a member of the Denver Board of Charities and Corrections and the State Board of Pardons, and campaigned for women's suffrage.

Channah Milstein, an East European immigrant and a former colonist at the failed Jewish agricultural colony in Cotopaxi, Colorado, was known for her extraordinary personal commitment to charity. For many years, she was a fixture on the landscape of Denver's west-side East European immigrant Jewish community as she relentlessly urged local residents to contribute to her collections for the needy.

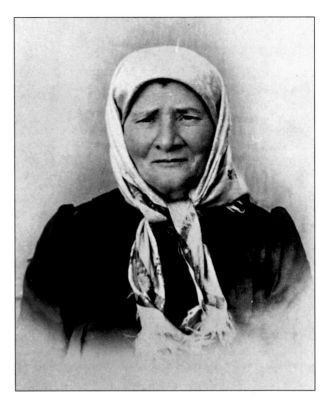

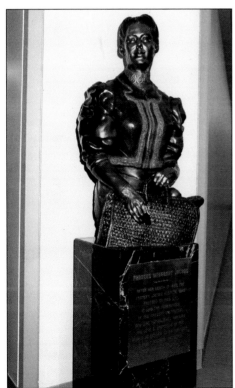

Frances Wisebart Jacobs became an icon of Denver philanthropy both within the Jewish and wider community. She made the treatment of tuberculosis victims her mission and was the impetus behind the founding of National Jewish Hospital. Active in a myriad of charitable activities, she was an officer of both the Hebrew Ladies' Benevolent Society and the general Denver Ladies' Benevolent Society, as well as a founder of Denver's first free kindergarten. In 1887, along with a Catholic priest and a Protestant minister, she helped organize the Charity Organization Society, a federation of Denver charitable organizations that evolved into the Community Chest and eventually became today's national United Way. This photograph depicts a bronze statue of Frances Wisebart Jacobs holding her famous bag of soaps and medicines. The statue stands in a central location in the lobby of the National Jewish Medical and Research Center, the successor to the NJH.

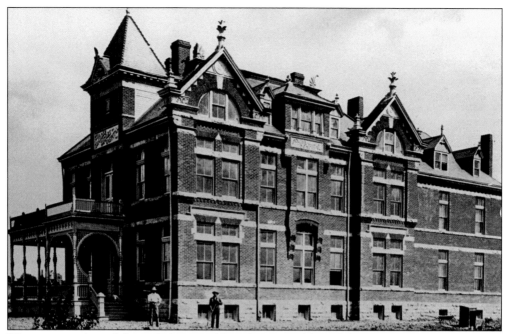

This exterior shot of the early National Jewish Hospital (NJH) features a sign over the front porch that reads "The Frances Jacobs Hospital." Because of economic challenges created in part by the Panic of 1893, the hospital was unable to open until 1899 when the national B'nai B'rith organization came to its aid with financial support. It was renamed National Jewish Hospital at that time. The NJH was founded and funded largely by affluent, Americanized German Reform Jews. It treated all patients free of charge under the motto "None May Enter Who Can Pay—None Can Pay Who Enter." However, the NJH admitted only patients with incipient tuberculosis and did not operate a kosher kitchen until 1923.

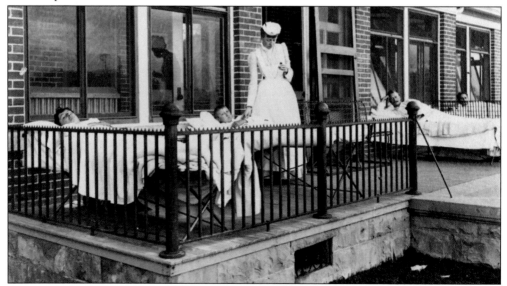

Open-air therapy was a cornerstone in tuberculosis treatment at the turn of the 20th century. In this 1907 photograph, male patients are lying in beds on the porch at the NJH as a nurse takes the temperature of one of the patients.

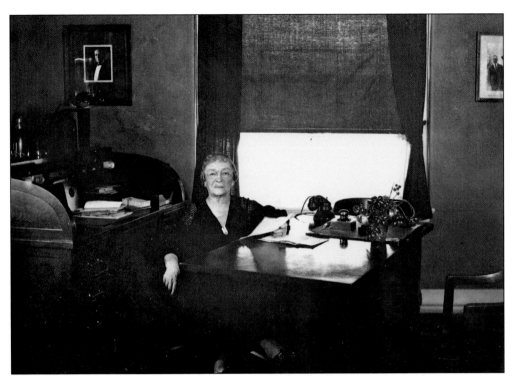

In the fluid social environment of the American West, many women were able to open new doors for themselves in the public sphere. Seraphine Eppstein Pisko was married to Denver Jewish pioneer businessman and politician Edward Pisko. Widowed at an early age, Seraphine became a prominent volunteer charity worker. When NJH opened in 1899, she accepted a job as a traveling fund-raiser for the institution. Her organizational skills and success as a fund-raiser pivoted her into the role of the executive secretary, or director of NJH, probably making her the first Jewish woman in America to head a national institution. In this c. 1922 picture, Seraphine is seated at her desk at NJH.

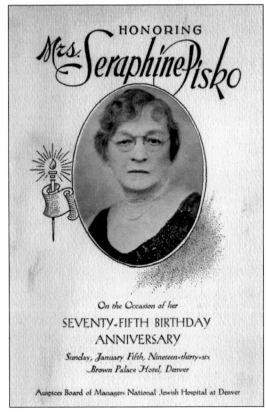

HONORING
Mrs. Seraphine Pisko

On the Occasion of her
SEVENTY-FIFTH BIRTHDAY
ANNIVERSARY
Sunday, January Fifth, Nineteen-thirty-six
Brown Palace Hotel, Denver

Auspices Board of Managers National Jewish Hospital at Denver

Seraphine Pisko was honored by NJH with a special dinner to celebrate her 75th birthday in 1936. Shown here is the front page of the dinner program.

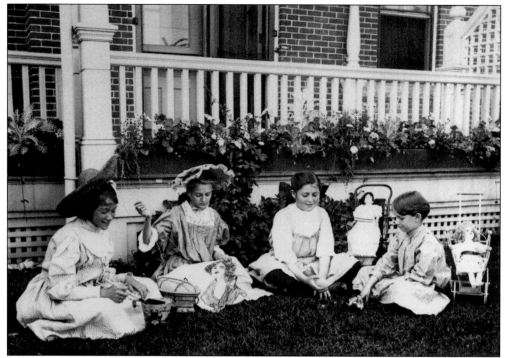

The National Jewish Hospital (NJH) worked to prevent tuberculosis by accepting children who seemed susceptible to the disease and offering good nutrition and plenty of fresh air to keep them healthy. This 1907 photograph shows four little girls seated on the lawn at NJH.

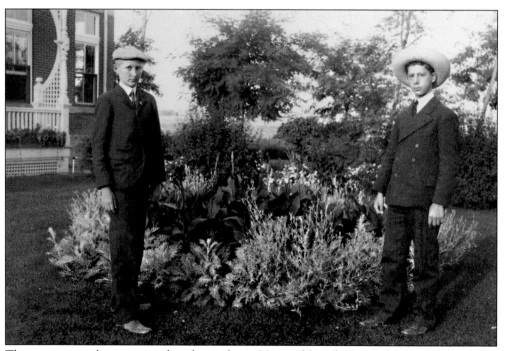

These two young boys are posed in the garden at National Jewish Hospital in 1907.

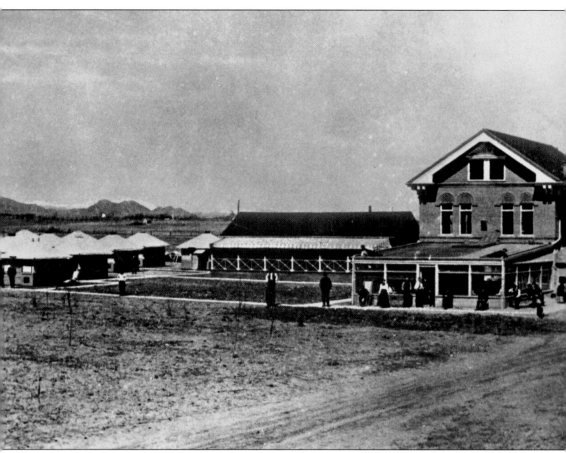

In 1903, a group of Jewish working class immigrants banded together to form the Jewish Consumptives' Relief Society (JCRS) to treat patients in all stages of the disease in a more Jewish environment and managed to raise $1.10 between them to launch the institution. They were joined by several prominent, local Jewish East European physicians, most notably Dr. Charles Spivak, who served as the executive secretary of the JCRS from 1904 until his death in 1927, and Dr. Philip Hillkowitz, who served as president of the JCRS from 1904 until his death in 1948. In 1904, the JCRS opened its doors. The JCRS motto was: "He who saves one life saves the world." This c. 1907 photograph shows the early buildings at the JCRS, including the famous tent cottages, built to give tuberculosis patients the maximum exposure to fresh air.

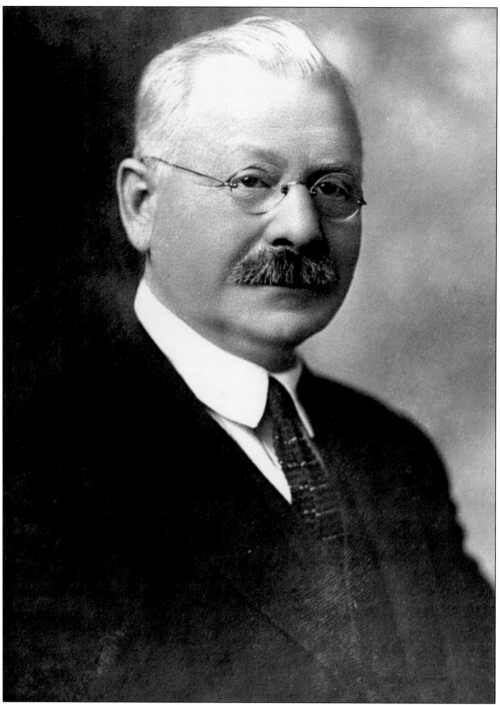

This formal portrait of Dr. Charles Spivak was taken c. 1920. Dr. Spivak, a Jewish immigrant who had fled Russia in 1881 because of his revolutionary socialist activities, received his medical degree from the Jefferson Medical College in Philadelphia in 1890. He and his family moved to Denver in 1896. Known as the "guiding genius" of the JCRS, he was referred to affectionately as "Papa Spivak" by his grateful patients.

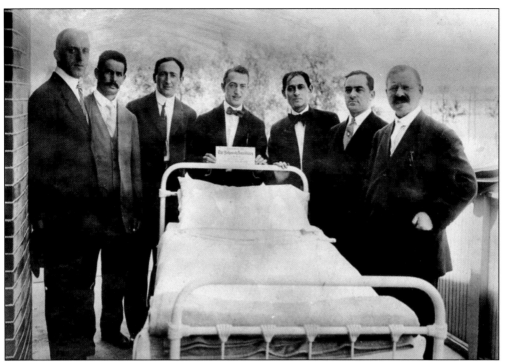

Many of the JCRS beds were sponsored by charitable contributions, including a number from JCRS women's auxiliaries located around the country. This photograph depicts the dedication of the Yehoash Auxiliary Bed by the Waterbury, Connecticut, group in 1911. Pictured from left to right are Dr. Herman Schwatt, then the JCRS medical director; Abraham Judelovitz, a Denver builder and JCRS volunteer; Dr. Philip Hillkowitz, longtime president of the JCRS; Ben Frumess; Yehoash (the Yiddish poet Solomon Bloomgarden); Mr. Kulp; and Dr. Charles Spivak.

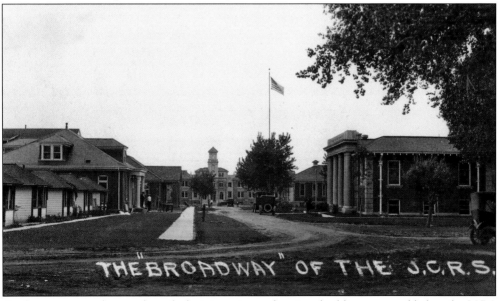

As the years passed, a number of administrative and patient buildings were added to the JCRS campus to treat an increasing number of consumptives.

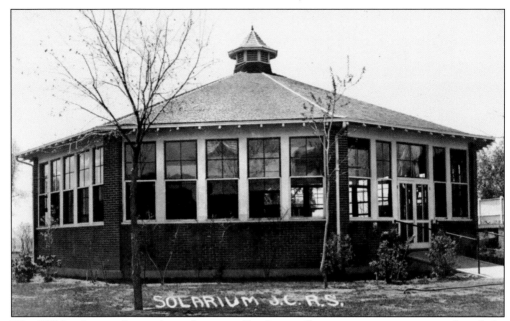

The JCRS solarium featured windows on all sides to allow a maximum amount of sunlight and fresh air.

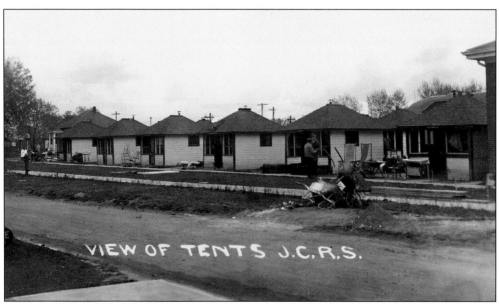

For many years, the JCRS featured both individual patient tent cottages, as well as indoor patient wards.

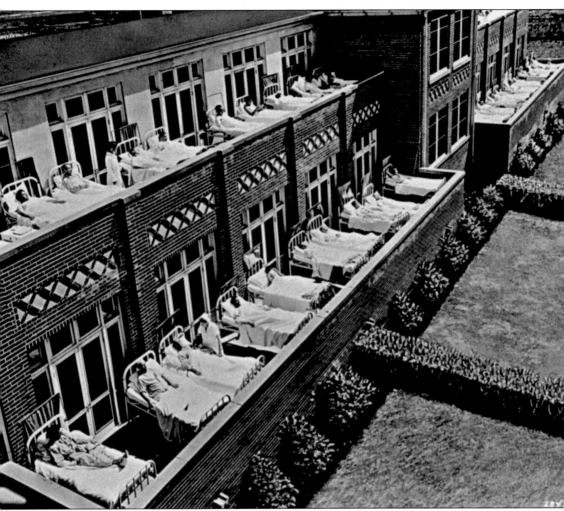

Heliotherapy, or maximum exposure to the sun, was considered part of an effective treatment for tuberculosis patients. Here patients are shown in beds pushed out onto the porches of the Texas Building at the JCRS.

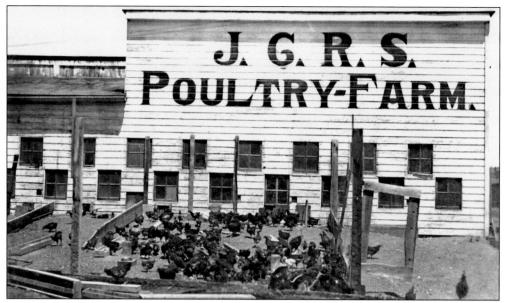

Fresh eggs, milk, and poultry were considered especially healthy for tuberculosis patients, who experts felt needed to be "built up" through nutritious, rich foods. The JCRS featured its own dairy and poultry farm located on its spacious grounds at the end of the Denver streetcar line in Lakewood, Colorado.

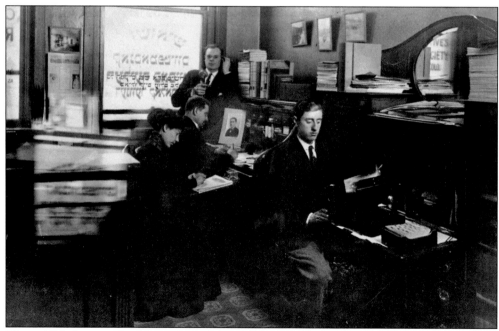

This c. 1915 photograph of the interior of the early JCRS business offices shows Dr. Charles Spivak seated at his desk (rear) and business manager Ben Friedland on the telephone.

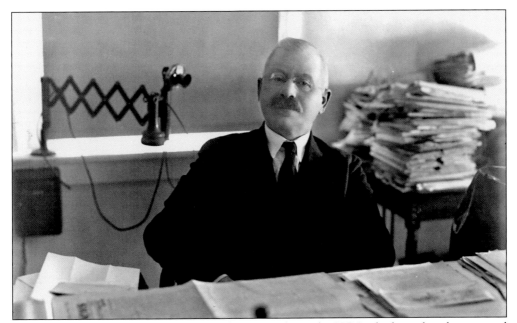

Dr. Charles Spivak's early socialist philosophy was in play at the JCRS, which was largely supported from modest donations by the members of the Jewish working class, most of them East European Jewish immigrants. He instructed one fund-raiser to collect money in dimes and quarters so the JCRS could continue as a "people's institution." In this photograph, Dr. Spivak is seated at his desk with a copy of the *Denver Jewish News* in front of him. He served as its first editor.

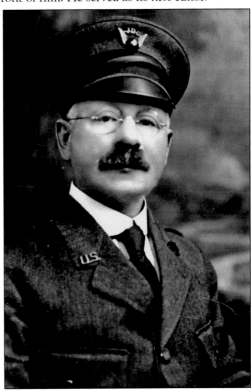

In 1920, Dr. Charles Spivak (pictured in uniform) took a leave of absence from the JCRS to serve as a special U.S. medical commissioner in war-torn Europe. He was officially a representative of the Jewish Distribution Committee to provide relief to Jewish refugees.

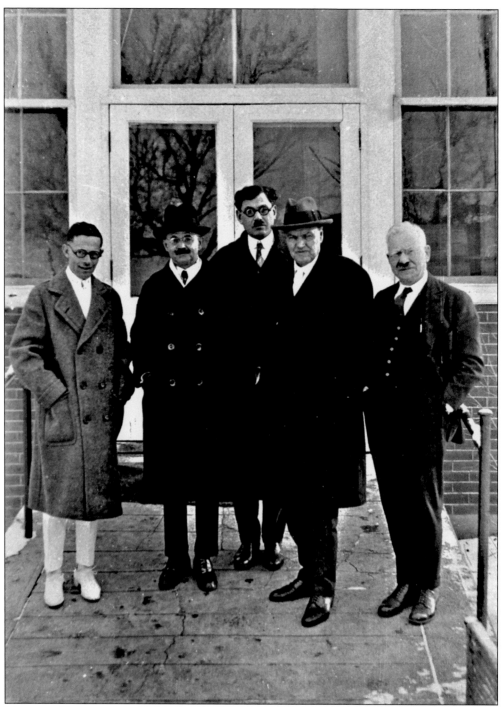

Many notables visited the JCRS, including famous American lawyer Clarence Darrow of Scopes trial fame. Darrow gave a speech to the patients on a visit to Denver in 1926. Pictured from left to right are Dr. Isidor Bronfin, JCRS medical superintendent, who later occupied the same position at NJH; Denver judge Ben Lindsey of the juvenile court; Dr. Leo Tepley; Clarence Darrow; and Dr. Charles Spivak.

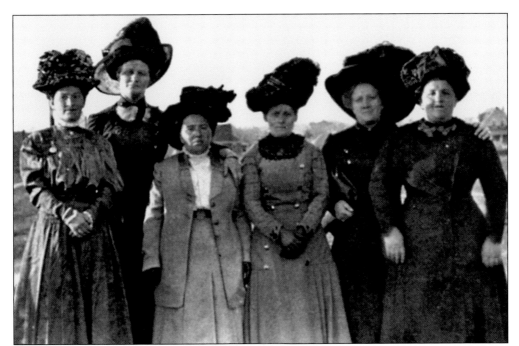

The Denver Sheltering Home for Jewish Children was founded in 1907 to care for children whose parents were victims of tuberculosis. It later evolved into the National Home for Asthmatic Children and eventually merged with National Jewish Hospital. Spearheaded by Fannie Lorber and Bessie Willens and other immigrant East European Jewish women, the home provided a traditional Jewish environment for the children who passed through its doors, as well as a strong secular education. Sadie Francis is pictured at the far right with Fannie Lorber to her left. Bessie Willens is shown third from the left.

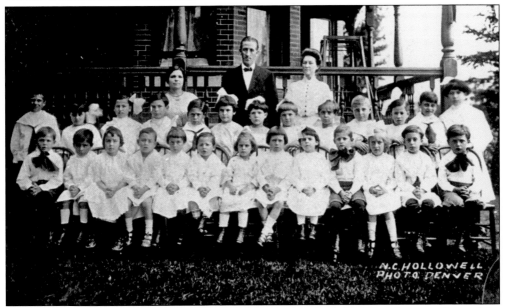

In this *c.* 1912 photograph, the early Denver Sheltering Home children are shown in front of the residence on Denver's west side with the matron and director.

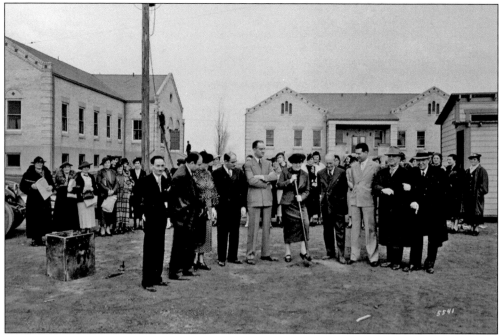

Fannie Lorber served as president of the Denver Sheltering Home for Jewish Children in all its iterations for more than 50 years, from 1907 until her death in 1958. When she died, the network of women's auxiliaries she had helped create nationally boasted more than 100,000 members. This photograph shows Fannie at the groundbreaking for the Lorber Building in 1937.

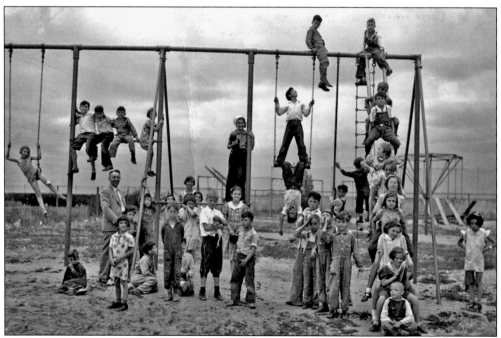

Pictured here are children on the playground at the National Home for Jewish Children, the former Denver Sheltering Home for Jewish Children, in the 1930s.

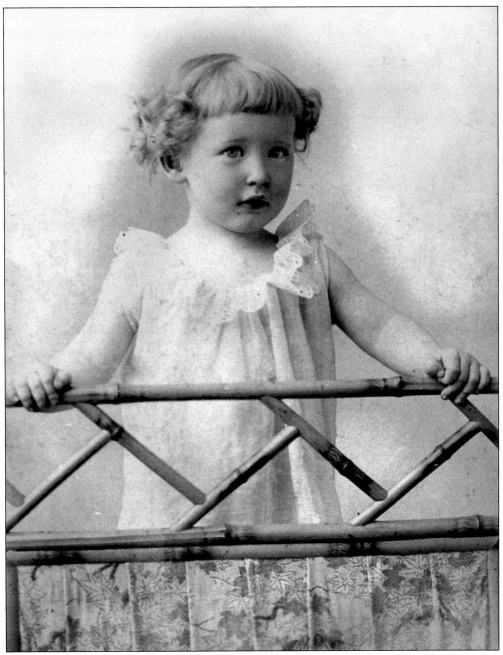

Tillye Shulman Levy, shown here at age two at the Shulman family home in Central City in 1897, became one of Denver's most active Jewish volunteers in the area of social welfare. Levy was inspired by Fannie Lorber, who encouraged the young woman to volunteer at the Denver Sheltering Home for Jewish Children. Levy later became a major force in the creation and development of what became the Jewish Family Service of Colorado.

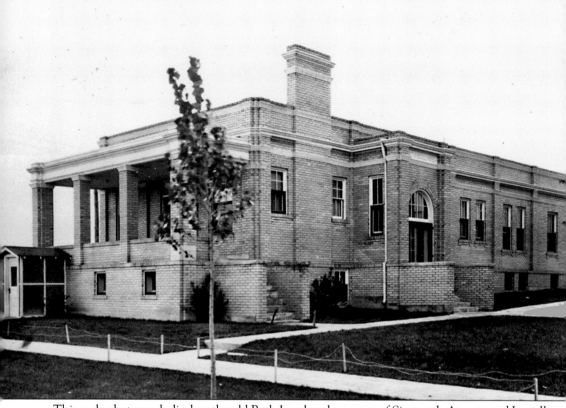

This early photograph displays the old Beth Israel at the corner of Sixteenth Avenue and Lowell Boulevard, which opened in Denver's west-side community in 1920 as a Jewish old-age home. It added a Jewish-run general hospital in 1923. Sparked by Bella Mintz, it garnered the support of members of Denver's Jewish community from throughout the city, and philanthropists Leopold Guldman, Isadore Rude, and Adolph Kiesler provided especially generous donations. Eventually, its geriatric center evolved into Denver's Shalom Park, located today in Aurora, Colorado, on the outskirts of south Denver.

Five

THE EAST EUROPEAN
NEWCOMERS

Denver's East European Jewish population began with a trickle in the 1870s, but this early group was soon augmented by a major influx of East European Jews in the 1880s, many part of a larger immigration fleeing increasing economic hardship and religious discrimination and attracted to the promise of new opportunities in America, the *Goldineh Medinah* or Golden Land. To alleviate the resulting problems of overcrowding and poverty in major eastern cities, some Jews were encouraged to go west. In 1882, fifty Russian immigrants arrived in Cotopaxi, Colorado, to pursue their dream of farming, an occupation long denied to them in their homeland. Within two years, the settlement was abandoned, and many of the colonists, including members of the Shames, Grimes, and Milstein families, made Denver their home, settling in the west-side immigrant enclave with other East European Jews.

Soon the area was filled with numerous small synagogues; small businesses, particularly those that catered to the mostly Orthodox Jewish immigrants (such as kosher bakeries, grocery stores, and meat markets); and many Jewish organizations. As more East European Jews arrived in Colorado, the influx produced a strain between the established, more Americanized Reform Jews and the newcomers with their traditional religious and cultural customs and sometimes radical political views. As the Russian Jews became successful and their American-educated children entered the professions, some moved into more substantial homes or into other, more affluent neighborhoods.

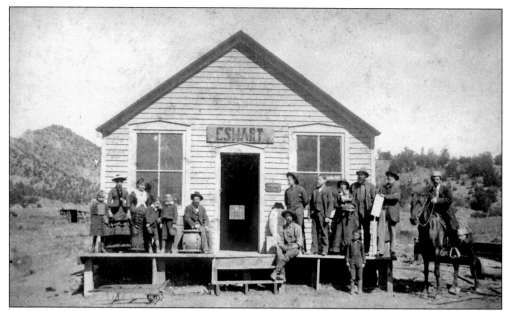

A number of the early Jewish Cotopaxi colonists are pictured here *c.* 1882 on the steps of the E. S. Hart Store. After the colony was disbanded, many moved to Denver, becoming active in the west-side immigrant Jewish community. (Courtesy of the American Jewish Historical Society.)

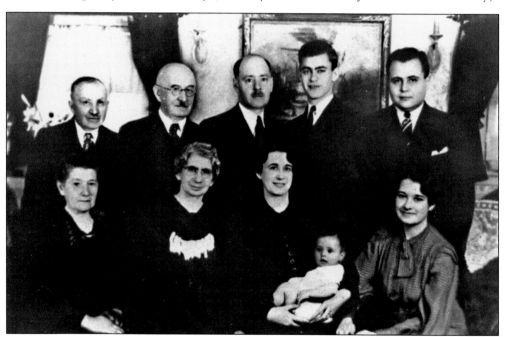

The Denver Quiat (Quiatkowsky) family began life in Colorado in Cotopaxi. Shown here at a family gathering are descendants of the Quiat family in 1935. Noted Denver attorney Simon Quiat is pictured standing in the back row, center. Pictured from left to right are (first row) Channah Quiat, Minnie Israelske, Pauline Quiat (Simon's wife), Loraine Friedman, and grandson Jerry Friedman on Pauline's lap; (second row) Fishel Quiat, Adolph Israelske, Simon Quiat, Harold Quiat, and Myer Friedman.

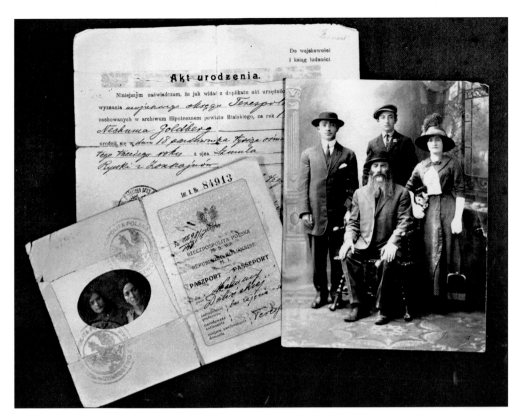

This photograph montage includes a portrait and immigration documents of the Dolinsky family, Jewish immigrants from Russian Poland who settled in Denver.

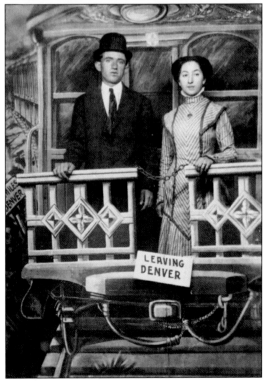

Abe and Rose Waldman Saliman are pictured here after their 1909 wedding in Denver. They were among the founders of the Hebrew Educational Alliance on Denver's west side. Abe was born in Denver in 1890, the son of Russian Jewish parents who had migrated to Denver in the late 1880s, while Rose was born in Russia and moved to Denver with her family in 1906. Abe later operated a restaurant with his brothers.

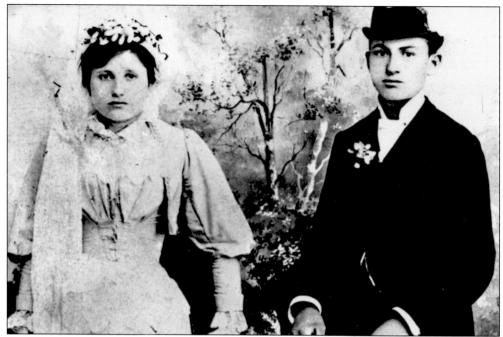

Sam and Anna Grimes were one of the early East European Jewish couples to be married in Denver. The wedding picture was taken in 1892.

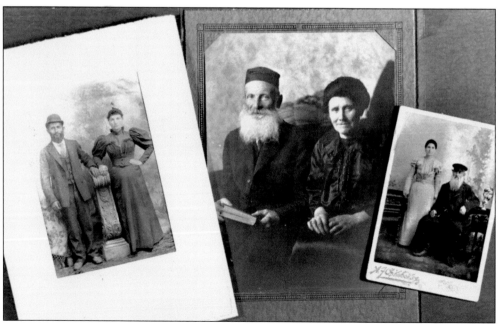

The Sunshine (left) and Feiner (center) families immigrated to Denver at the beginning of the 20th century. While some of Jacob Sarnoff Ginsberg's children made Denver their permanent home, Jacob (pictured at right with his wife) returned to Russia before World War I.

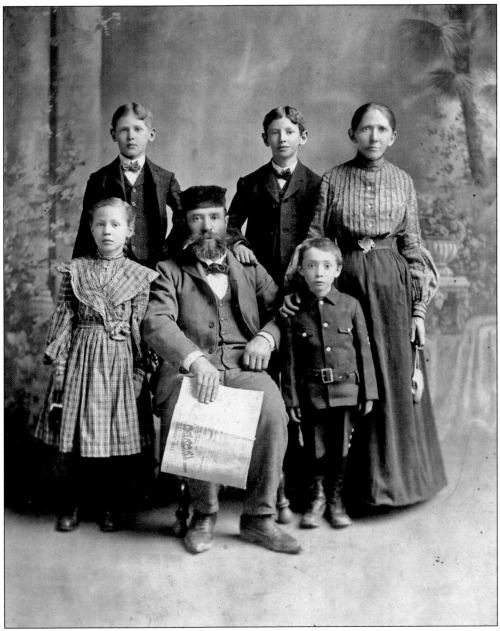

This *c.* 1907 studio portrait of East European Jewish immigrants Joseph and Nettie Goldfain and their children shows the family in Denver with Joseph holding a Yiddish newspaper printed in America. Pictured from left to right are (first row) Rose, Joseph, and Ephraim Goldfain; (second row) George, Samuel, and Nettie Goldfain.

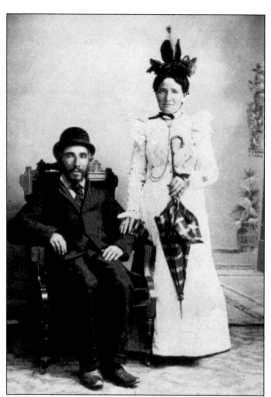

The Kortz family originated in Brest Litovsk, Russia, and arrived in Denver around 1885. Pictured here are Israel and Rebecca Kortz in Denver c. 1900. The Kortz family and their descendants have contributed to the development of Denver and its Jewish community for six generations.

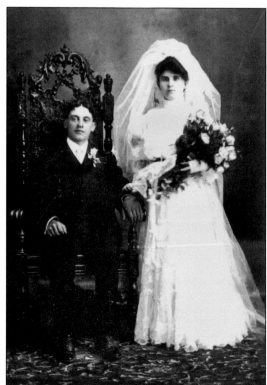

East European immigrants Max and Anna Schatz Rosenthal were married in Denver in 1906 and raised their family there.

The Averch family arrived in Denver from Eastern Europe around the turn of the 20th century and lived under the Colfax viaduct on Denver's west side. Morris Averch ran the Capitol Meat Packing Company. Morris and Zelda Averch are pictured here with their children Anna Averch Kaminsky and Meyer and Dave Averch around 1908.

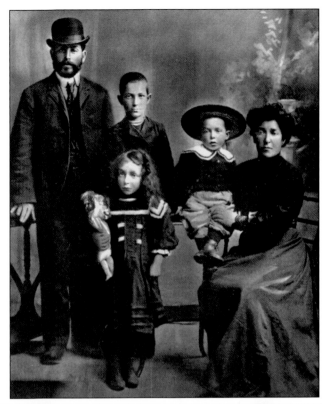

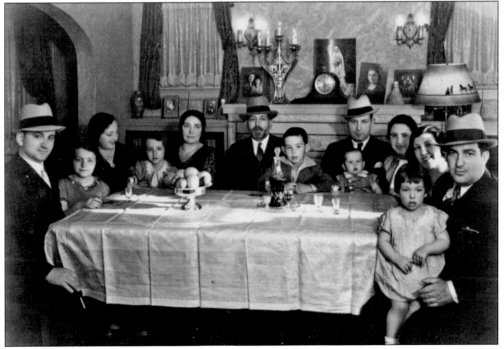

In 1932, the Morris and Zelda Averch family celebrated the Passover Seder with their children and grandchildren, including members of the Kaminsky family.

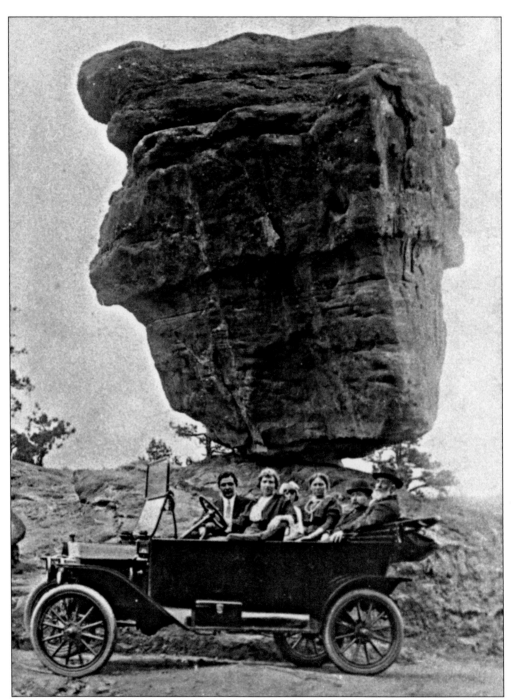

Morris and Anna Ginsberg Hayutin are shown here *c.* 1914 with Max and D'vera Ginsberg and other family members on an outing to Balanced Rock, near Colorado Springs, Colorado. The Ginsberg family settled on Denver's west side in 1910, and they became an active part of the Orthodox Jewish community where they were known for their hospitality, always providing a bed and meals for visitors. Max prospered in an auto-wrecking and metal business and was a founding member of Congregation Zere Israel.

Anna Ginsberg Hayutin was born in Russia but came to New York City with her parents, D'vera and Max Ginsberg, as a young child and moved to Denver in 1910. Anna married the son of Russian immigrants, businessman Morris Hayutin, who owned the Western Supply Company and later the Public Industrial Bank.

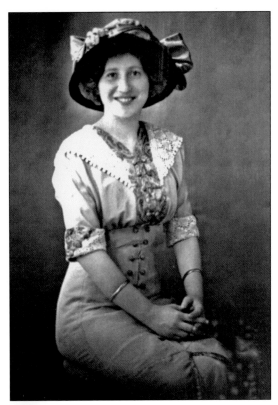

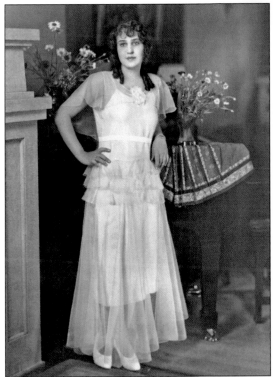

This portrait of Peryle Hayutin Beck was taken on her 16th birthday in Denver in 1931. Peryle was the daughter of Morris and Anna Ginsberg Hayutin. She married businessman Ira M. Beck in 1935 and later received a master's degree in speech from the University of Denver. Peryle Beck founded the Beck Archives in 1976 in memory of her husband.

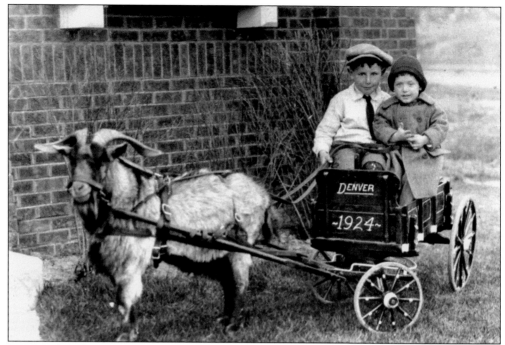

Irving and Arthur Hayutin are pictured here as children in a goat-drawn cart near their childhood home on Denver's west side in 1924. Irving and Arthur, who both became attorneys, were the sons of Morris and Anna Ginsberg Hayutin.

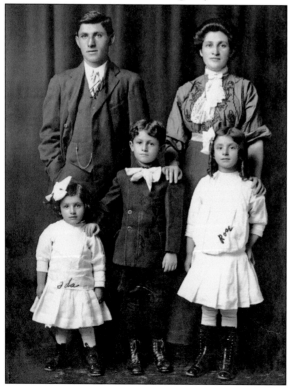

Pictured here around 1913, Gedalia (George) and Minnie Toltz and their children Ida, Israel, and Rose became active members of the west-side East European Jewish community. Ida's married name became Radetsky, and Rose's became Mizel.

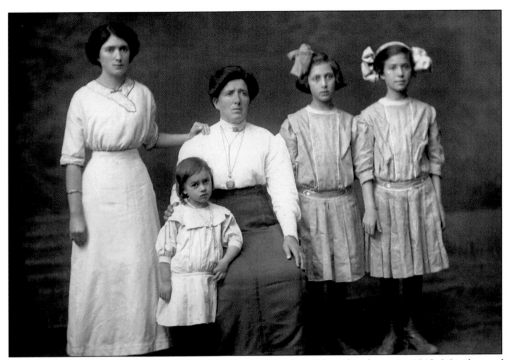

Pictured here are Rachel Sosne (Mrs. Abraham Sosne) and her daughters in 1913. Members of the Sosne family ran the Capitol Wet Wash Laundry on West Colfax Avenue.

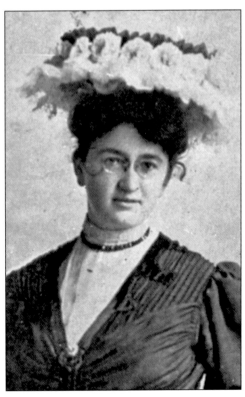

Anna Hillkowitz was born in Russia, the daughter of Rabbi Elias and Rebecca Hillkowitz and sister of Dr. Philip Hillkowitz, longtime president of the JCRS. Anna entered library school after high school graduation and took a position as a librarian with the Denver public library. Highly active in the Denver Jewish community, she took a leave of absence from her job in 1907 to work as a successful traveling fund-raiser for the JCRS. She traveled to more than 40 cities in her first six months on the job.

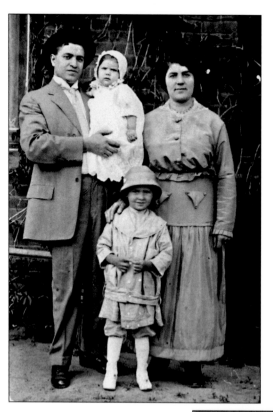

East European Jewish immigrants Sam and Bertha Flax started out married life in Cripple Creek, Colorado, but moved to Denver in the early part of the 20th century so their two sons, baby Leo and Isidor, could grow up in a larger Jewish community.

Immigrants Abraham and Miriam (Mary) Kobey began their life in Colorado in Central City. The devout couple became vegetarians for a time while living there because kosher meat transported from Denver often arrived spoiled. After they moved to Denver, Abraham worked as a rabbi and *sofer*, or scribe, and Miriam became a busy and highly respected midwife, often performing her services free for poor women. She is shown here with several of her Kobey grandchildren in Aspen, Colorado.

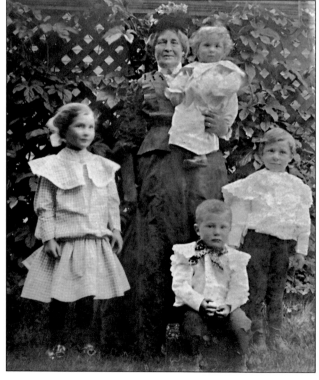

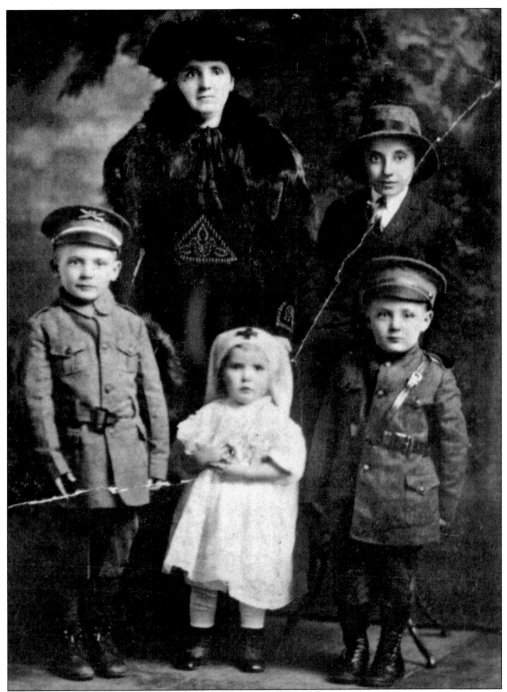

Jacob Mosko, a blacksmith, arrived in Denver in 1905, and within a few years, he sent for his wife and the six children who had been born in Eastern Europe. Pictured here are his wife, Ida Mosko, and the four other children in the family who were born in America. The small girl dressed in a miniature nurse's uniform was the family's youngest child Ruth, who grew up in Denver. Born in 1916, Ruth later married Izzy Elliot Handler, and the two cofounded the enormously successful Mattel Toy Company. The famous Barbie doll was Ruth's creation.

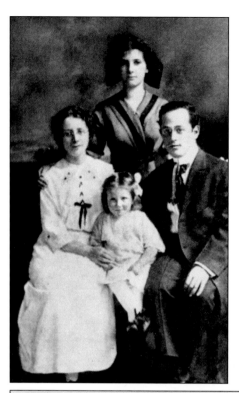

Future Israeli prime minister Golda Meir (standing, center) is pictured here with her sister and brother-in-law, Shana and Sam Korngold, and their daughter Judy. The picture was taken in Denver in 1914. A teenaged Golda lived with the Korngolds for about a year and a half in Denver's west-side immigrant Jewish community and attended North High School. Shana had suffered from tuberculosis and had been a patient at both National Jewish Hospital and the Jewish Consumptives' Relief Society sanatorium. The time Golda spent in Denver was pivotal because she first learned about democratic socialism through late night gatherings at her sister's house, and it was in Denver that she met and was courted by her future husband, Morris Myerson. (Courtesy of the Golda Meir House, Auraria Foundation.)

Telegram

western union

```
FT0192 KIT956 JTA142 2051 1126458
UINX CY ILJM 096
JERUSALEM ISRAEL 96 28 1600 ETATDISRAEL


RICHARD N. BLUESTEIN  NATIONAL JEWISH HOSPITAL AND RESEARCH
CENTER 3800 EAST COLFAX AVENUE
DENVER COLORADO
I READILY JOIN IN EXTENDING CONGRATULATIONS TO THE NATIONAL
JEWISH HOSPITAL AND RESEARCH CENTER ON ITS SEVENTY FIFTH ANNIVERSARY
STOP MY MEMORY OF THE HOSPITAL GOES BACK TO THE YEAR 1908 WHEN MY
DEAR SISTER OF BLESSED MEMORY SHANA BENEFITED FROM THE HOSPITAL'S
TREATMENT STOP I SALUTE THE THREE QUARTERS OF A CENTURY OF THE
HOSPITAL'S HUMAN SERVICE AND SCIENTIFIC ACHIEVEMENT CARRIED OUT IN
THE BEST JEWISH TRADITION OF DEVOTION TO THE WELFARE OF OUR
FELLOWMEN STOP MAY THE ENTERPRISE ENJOY CONTINUED SUCCESS

     GOLDA MEIR

COL ETATDISRAEL 3800EAST 1908
NNN
NNNN
```

Prime minister of Israel Golda Meir sent this telegram to National Jewish Hospital in 1974 congratulating the institution on its 75th anniversary and thanking them for the care that had been provided to her sister.

Ellis and Bessie Ruttman Wedgle were married in Denver in 1914 after a brief courtship. The two arrived in the United States about 1912, Ellis emigrating from Poland and Bessie from Russia. In Denver, Ellis worked as a pawnbroker, and Bessie was a seamstress. They lived in Denver's west-side immigrant community and raised four children there.

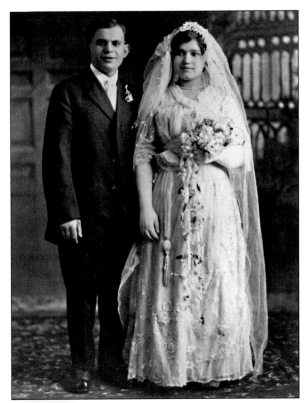

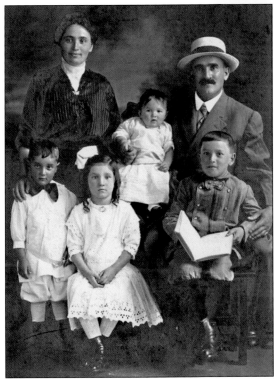

Harry and Rose Battock are pictured here in 1921 with four (Ben, Sophie, Joe, and Mary) of their eventual six children. Harry, who came to Denver to be treated at the JCRS, peddled fruit and vegetables from a horse-drawn wagon on Denver's west side.

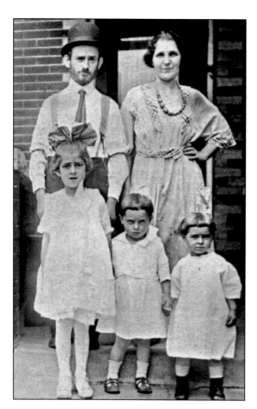

Jacob and Charlotte Gorden are pictured here c. 1920 with their daughters Bess, Baila, and Eleanor. Jacob, a *schohet*, Talmudic scholar, and later a *mohel*, migrated to Denver in 1914 from Russia to join his uncle, Velvel Heller. Soon Jacob had saved enough to bring his wife and daughter over, and the family settled on the Denver's west side. Two more daughters and a son were born in the family.

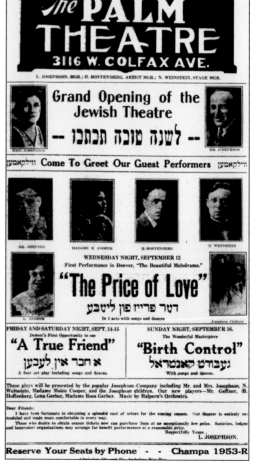

From 1922 to 1926, the Jewish Theatrical Company, organized by the Josephson family, ran a Yiddish theater at the Palm Theatre on West Colfax Avenue in the East European immigrant enclave. This poster advertised the grand opening of their enterprise.

Etta Miller Robinson was born in Lithuania and was the eldest daughter of cattle dealer Robert Lazar Miller. Etta married Hyman Robinson, who ran his family's dairy business with his brother Morris. Tragically, Etta died in childbirth in 1900 when the couple's son Sam was born. Sam Robinson was responsible for the transformation of the Robinson Farm Climax Dairy into the Gold Seal Dairy, which later became Robinson Dairy.

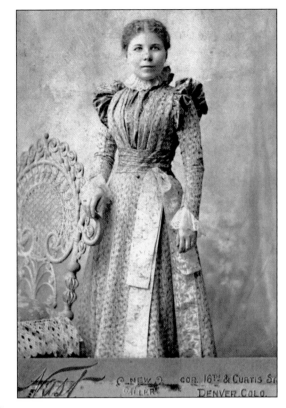

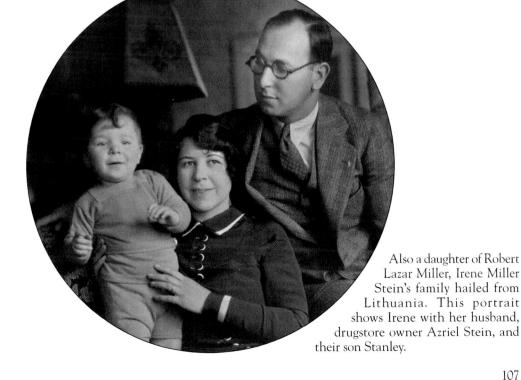

Also a daughter of Robert Lazar Miller, Irene Miller Stein's family hailed from Lithuania. This portrait shows Irene with her husband, drugstore owner Azriel Stein, and their son Stanley.

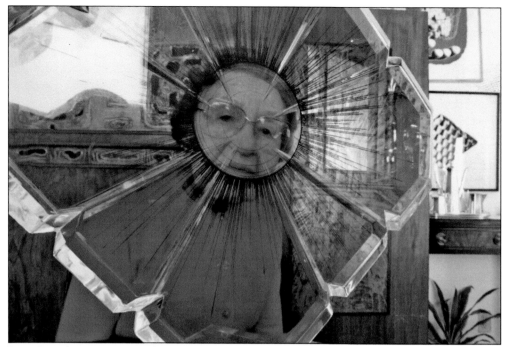

Irene Stein became a regional artist of note in a variety of media and was still producing innovative works into her 90s. She is shown here with one of her glass pieces.

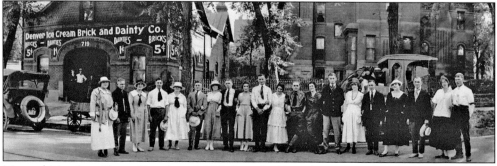

Mr. and Mrs. Joe Alpert (fourth and fifth from left) are shown here at a social outing with their friends in Denver in 1917. Joe Alpert became an active supporter of Beth Israel Hospital and Geriatric Center.

Six

Jewish Communities Outside of Denver

With the coming of the railroads, Denver's position as Colorado's leading city was cemented. Still, pockets of Jewish populations could be found in almost all of Colorado's towns and hamlets where Jews held well-respected business and social reputations. In the tiny mining town of Fairplay, for example, although the Cohens were the only Jewish family residing there, pioneer Samuel Cohen was elected mayor. While the mining towns prospered, so did the Jewish merchants and shopkeepers. However, as Denver became Colorado's predominant city, most Jews in settlements throughout the state moved to the "Queen City" and other larger Colorado communities like Colorado Springs and Boulder. A minority remained in small towns like Fort Collins, Greeley, and Longmont where their small establishments flourished for many years.

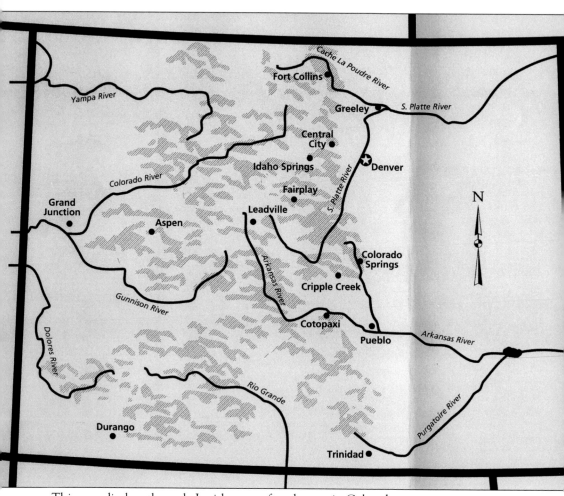

This map displays the early Jewish areas of settlement in Colorado.

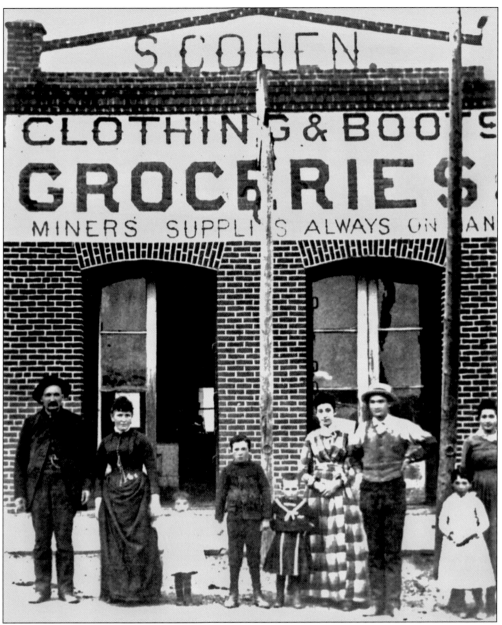

This photograph shows Cohen family members standing in front of their general store in Fairplay, Colorado. Pictured from left to right are Samuel, Eva, Pearl, Harry, Louis, Phoebe, Joseph, Gustave, and Amelia. Merchant Sam Cohen was elected mayor of Fairplay and was also a state representative from Park County in 1898. He helped write Colorado's mining legislation.

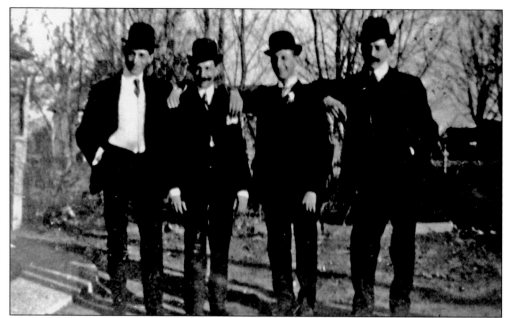

Morris Meyer came to Colorado in the 1890s to cure his tuberculosis and founded the Golden Rule Dry Goods Store in Rocky Ford. At one time, there were seven flourishing Meyer Stores operating in Northern Colorado. Pictured here *c.* 1908 are the four Meyer brothers, from left to right, Charles, Morris, Sam, and Max.

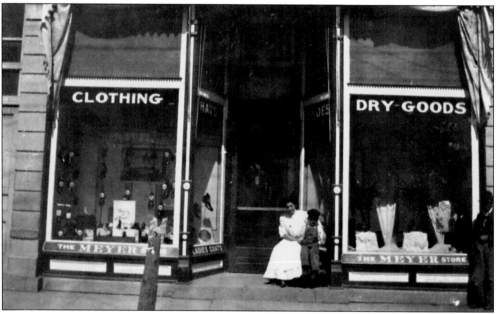

As a young immigrant from Poland, Sam Meyer established the Meyer Store in 1905, a dry goods and apparel business in Fort Collins. He later opened branches in Windsor, Loveland, and Fort Morgan. Ida and Sam Meyer were married in 1908, and both became active in the town's civic and social life. They became members of Denver's Temple Emanuel and raised funds in Fort Collins for the NJH and the JCRS. Ida and an unidentified boy are pictured here in front of the Meyer Store in Fort Collins in 1908.

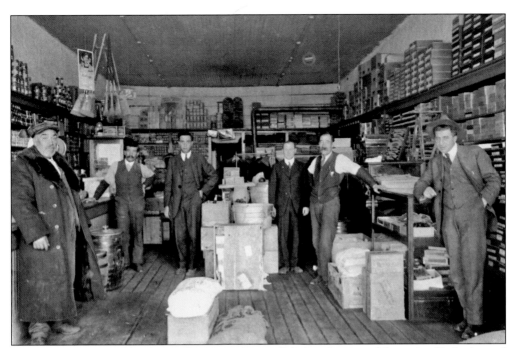

Edward Green opened his dry goods store in the small Colorado town of Antonito. He is pictured at the far right leaning on the counter.

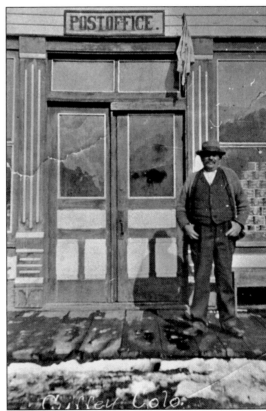

Gus Cohen served as the postmaster and a justice of the peace in the hamlet of Guffey, Colorado.

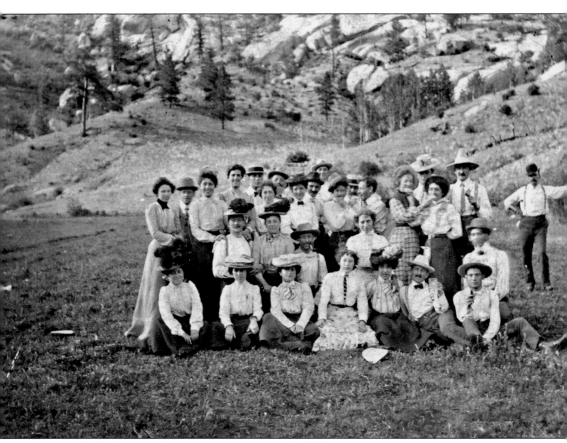

Cripple Creek was a thriving mining town in the 1890s with an active Jewish community. Many Jewish merchants established themselves in Cripple Creek, Jewish religious services were held regularly, and a B'nai B'rith chapter was founded in 1901. After mining petered out in the area in the early years of the 20th century, most Jews moved to Denver. Pictured here is a group of early Jewish residents gathered for a social outing in the 1890s.

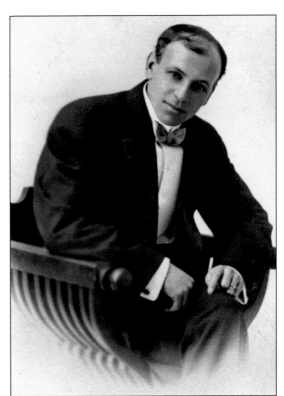

Shown here are portraits of Harry
and Minnie Harris of Cripple
Creek. Harry served as postmaster
in Cripple Creek in the 1890s. The
couple later moved to Denver where
Harry operated a coal company.

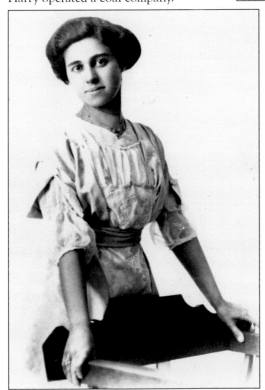

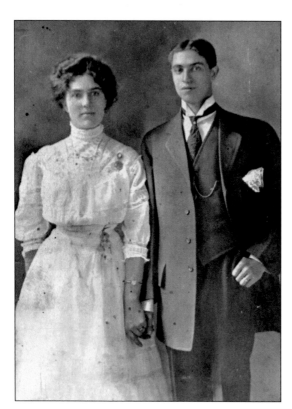

Sam and Bertha Flax were married in Cripple Creek c. 1909. Unsuited for life as a miner, Sam worked in a local saloon before the couple moved to Denver where he became a successful businessman.

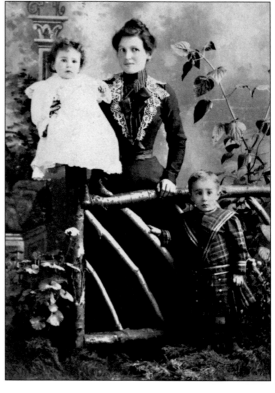

Leadville, Colorado, boomed in the late 19th century after a rich silver strike. At the peak of the mining frenzy, the town attracted a large Jewish population made up primarily of merchants and professionals and their families. Twenty-three Jewish-owned clothing and dry goods stores graced Leadville's streets in 1881. Pictured here are Celia Stager Isaacs and her children Sadie and Louis in 1901.

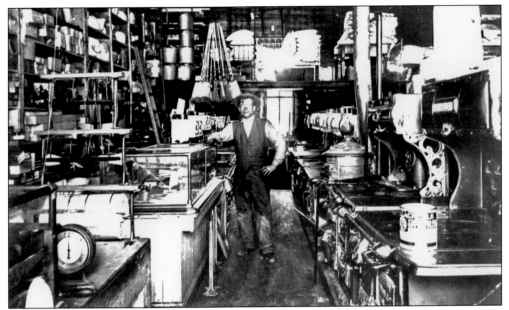

Shown here c. 1900 is the interior of the Isaacs Hardware Store in Leadville.

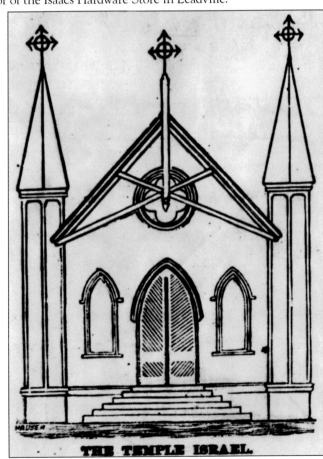

THE TEMPLE ISRAEL.

In its heyday, Leadville boasted two synagogues. Pictured here is a drawing of the Reform Temple Israel. The congregation was formed in 1884. The Orthodox congregation Kneseth Israel was organized in 1892. (Courtesy of the Denver Public Library, Western History Collection.)

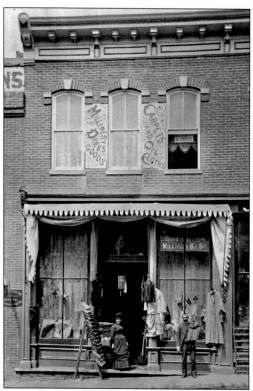

Central City was a booming mining town by 1860, soon after gold was discovered along Clear Creek. Jews settled in Central City from the beginning. Pioneer Abraham Rittmaster's early store was bought out by his nephew Abraham Rachofsky, who became one of the city's most important businessmen. Pictured here c. 1890 is Rachofsky's New York Store.

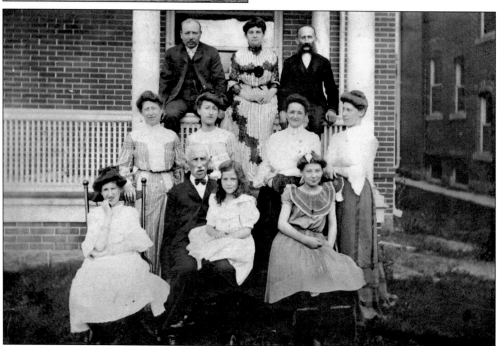

Robert Shulman (seated back row, left) ran a clothing store in Central City. He is pictured here in the late 1890s with visitors and his wife and in-laws, the Saly family. Michael Saly (seat back row, right) was a founder of Denver's Jewish Mount Nebo Cemetery.

Long before Aspen, Colorado, was known as a ski resort, it was a mining town. The Bavarian-born lawyer David Hyman became a major investor in mining properties there and helped establish the town in 1880. One of Aspen's main streets was named Hyman Avenue in his honor.

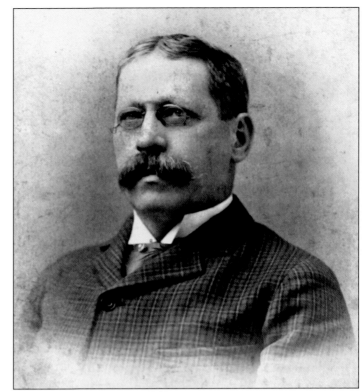

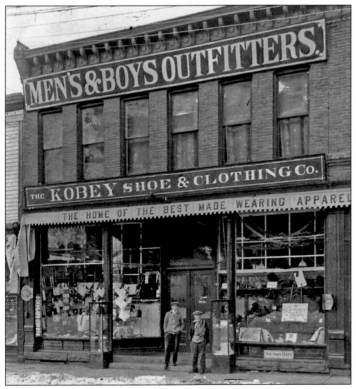

A number of Jewish merchants moved to Aspen to take advantage of business opportunities. This picture shows Kobey's Shoe and Clothing Store, which was in business from the late 1880s to the early 1930s. Leah Kobey died in 1920, but Harris Kobey and their six children lived in Aspen until 1924.

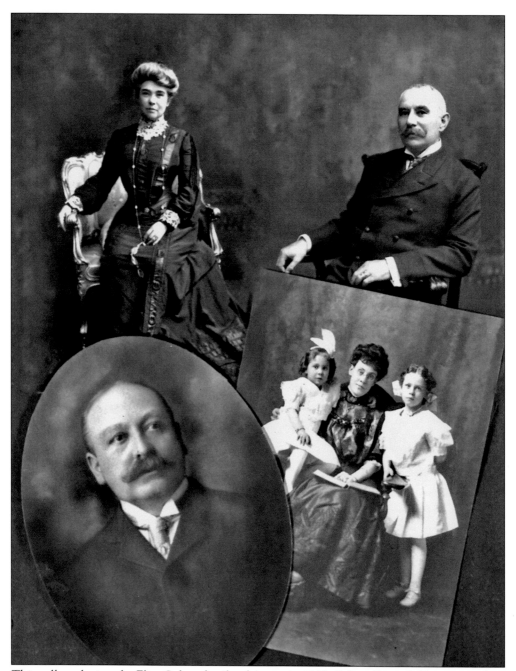

This collage depicts the Elias Cohen family of Aspen in 1905. Cohen (lower left) was a resident of Aspen by 1891 and managed David Hyman's properties. It was Cohen who suggested the use of deep-sea divers to repair broken mine-pump shafts. His wife and daughters appear at the bottom right, and his wife's parents, the Weinbergs, are shown at the top of the photograph.

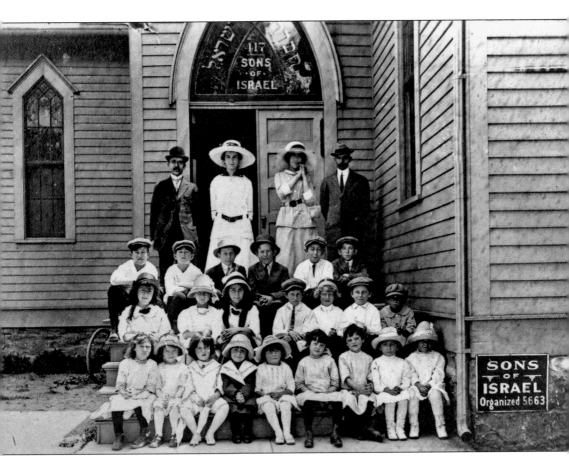

Colorado Springs was the site of a growing Jewish community. Congregation Sons of Israel was organized in 1903. Pictured here are members of the Hebrew School around 1915 with their two female teachers, May Myers (left) and May Margaret Golin (right).

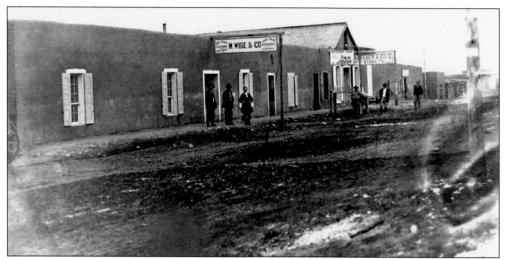

Maurice Wise may have been the first Jewish merchant in Trinidad, Colorado. Pictured here c. 1870 is the exterior of the M. Wise and Company dry goods store. (Courtesy of the Colorado Historical Society.)

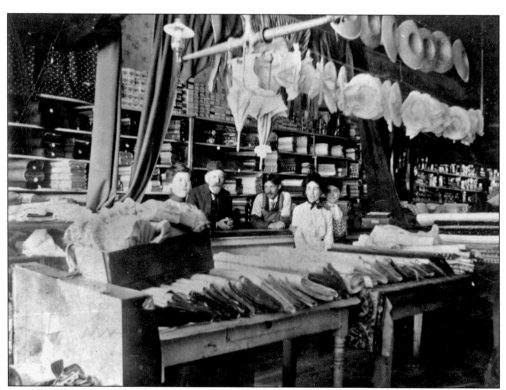

By 1900, Trinidad was a bustling commercial center serving the surrounding mining district. Seventy Jews made the city their home at the time, mostly merchant families of German and East European extraction. Brothers Henry, Sol, and Sam Jaffa were in Trinidad by the 1870s. Pictured here c. 1890 is the interior of the Jaffa Mercantile Company. (Courtesy of the American Jewish Archives.)

The Sanders brothers, Simon, Joseph, and Jacob, were wholesale liquor dealers and leaders of Congregation Aaron. This c. 1885 portrait of Jennie and Simon Sanders was taken in Trinidad, Colorado.

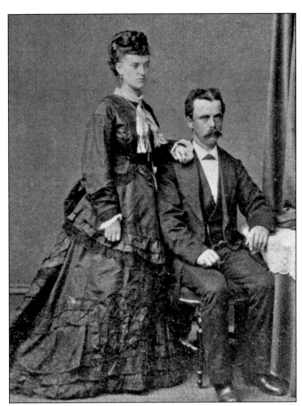

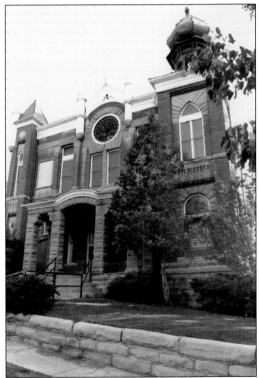

Temple Aaron of Trinidad was organized in 1883, and the congregation erected this elaborate brick building, still standing today, in 1889. There was a *minyan* for the Jewish holiday of *Rosh Hashonah* in Trinidad as early as 1872.

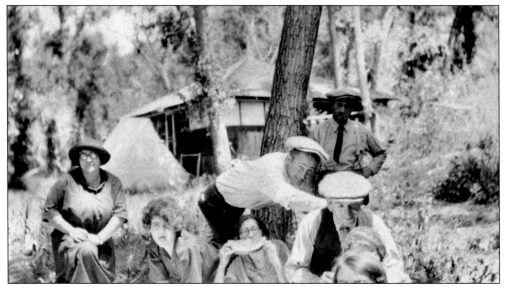

Greeley, Colorado, featured a modest Jewish population in the early part of the 20th century, mostly Orthodox Jews. Congregation Beth Israel was incorporated in 1925. Abe Winograd was one of the early leaders of the community and established a poultry business after trying his hand at peddling. The small group of early Greeley Jews had an active social life. Pictured here is the annual picnic of the Hebrew Progressive Club held in 1921.

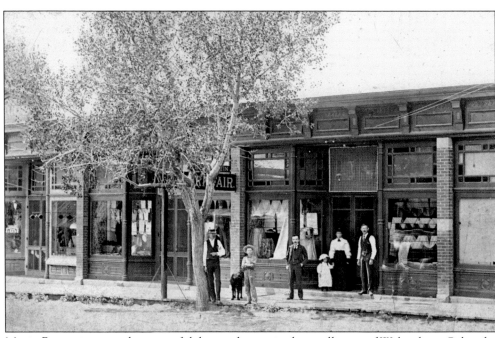

Moritz Bernstein opened a successful dry goods store in the small town of Walsenberg, Colorado. He is pictured here *c.* 1895 in front of his store.

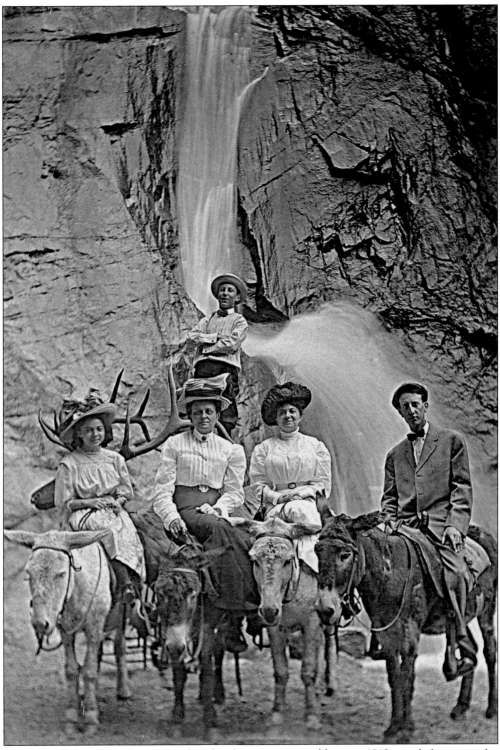

Members of the Bernstein family of Walsenberg are pictured here in 1910 astride burros at the famous scenic site of Seven Falls, Colorado.

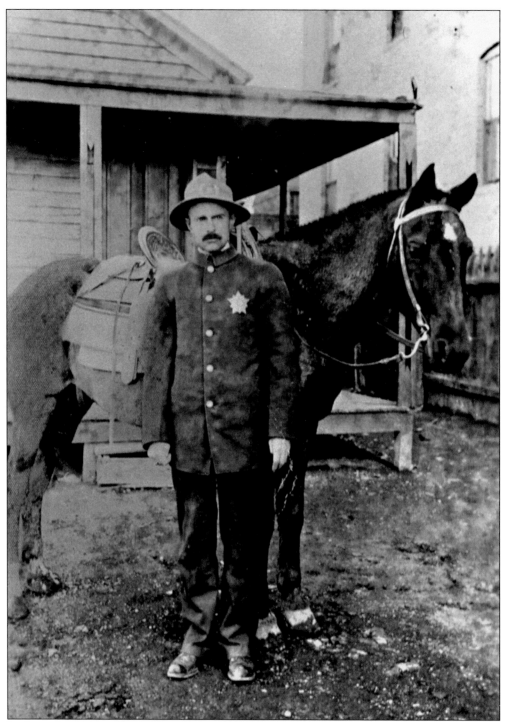

In the industrial city of Pueblo, Colorado, the "Steel City of the West," a Jewish *minyan* was held as early as 1880, and a B'nai B'rith chapter was founded in 1882. Later both traditional and reform congregations were organized. Many Pueblo Jews started as peddlers and became merchants. Max Stein, an early Jewish Pueblo resident, is pictured here *c*. 1910 as a mounted policeman.

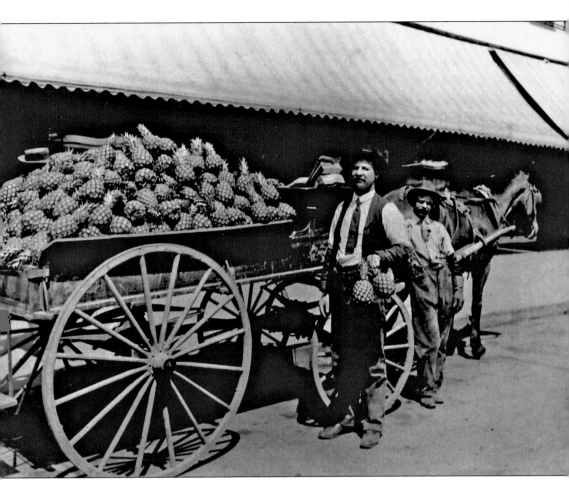

Max Stein became a peddler and successful businessman. He is shown here in front of his wagon selling pineapples in Pueblo around 1915.

DISCOVER THOUSANDS OF LOCAL HISTORY BOOKS FEATURING MILLIONS OF VINTAGE IMAGES

Arcadia Publishing, the leading local history publisher in the United States, is committed to making history accessible and meaningful through publishing books that celebrate and preserve the heritage of America's people and places.

Find more books like this at
www.arcadiapublishing.com

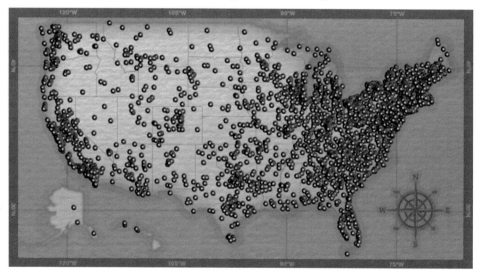

Search for your hometown history, your old stomping grounds, and even your favorite sports team.

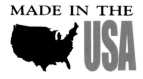